# Practical Algorithms
## Third Edition

ISBN-13: 978-1500173456

ISBN-10: 1500173452

# Contents

Contents
Practical Algorithms

# Unit 7—Database Design ...................................................119

# Foreword

No two logicians can agree on a definition for logic.

—Bertrand Russell

At a minimum, algorithms is an upper division subject. Ideally it is a graduate-level course for computer engineers and project managers. Gaming theory is an entirely separate subject that could be taken simultaneously with this course, but does not belong in this course. Both belong in the computer science division of a math department, not the information technology division of a business department. The materials provided here were designed for an upper division course requiring only the introductory computer class, but were also used inappropriately and prematurely in a community college that thought it should also contain gaming theory (a thought I ignored).

The choice of materials here is unique for several reasons. First, algorithms is about solving classes of problems. While pseudocode is included for the sake of literacy, it does nothing to solve real problems. As a consultant it was my job to actually solve problems, and the first one was establishing the problem in a meeting with those who used pseudocode, and the pseudocode played no role in that process. Second, marketable skill create academic integrity, not difficulty. As an academic dean, I taught virtually every subject and was responsible for the curriculum of literally every class. Algorithms was the most difficult class for both students and instructors, and no college or university seemed to know what the course really meant or how difficult it was. It needed simplifying into practical marketable skills.

Tasked with making the course work at one university, I poured over the available textbooks with grave disappointment. I had a mountain of classroom-tested materials available, so I put them together into this book. My choice in materials was partly guided by MCSE, MCSD, and A+ requirements, and partly guided by experience both in the field and the classroom. I decided the best thing I could do was teach the students how to think, how to interface with both subjective business requirements and objective resources, and be practical problem solvers who provided scalable solutions. It was not my job to teach a programming language or math skills in this course. This gave administration at every college the misconception that these were not needed prior to taking the class. Having seen universities put trigonometry before algebra and nuclear decay before periodic table basics, this was no surprise. It was my job to produce marketable graduates, not drive them out of classes with unreasonable expectations. Unlike most classes, students taking algorithms or gaming theory have a significant and specific career goal requiring the subject. This class is not for general audiences, and if the school cannot fit it correctly into its curriculum, they shouldn't offer it. It does not belong in any two-year school.

I made many important innovations for this book. The most significant was expanding the subjective elements of Microsoft's programs by teaching sales, analysis, and proposal skills. As a consultant I regularly had to clean up the messes of previous consultants. The most common mess was failure to lock in the expectations and requirements of the project. The next most common mess was solving the "unsolvable" which is code for "unsolved." The point of algorithms is to find such object-oriented solutions, not to rely on some rapid aided design technology. If RAD is all you need, then you really don't need the algorithms class. Solving the unsolved meant teaching the tools used for such tasks like flowcharting and symbolic logic. Since pseudocode and flowcharting are virtually incompatible and C++ is intuitively simple, I primarily used C++. Years earlier I tackled Russell's issue of logic (above), having distilled and established a mathematically consistent system of practical symbolic logic. This had proven helpful over the years in a variety of applications, from the classroom to solving cutting edge cosmology problems.

It may seem strange to some for a programmer to take on cosmology problems. Computers were an awkward tool when I began working with them. You had to program to accomplish anything. Even printers came without drivers, so you had to work out the machine language without instructions. As soon as I could walk away from programming, I did. It followed me and put food on the table, so I welcomed a host of certifications I had no personal interest in and priced myself out of the market before I could enjoy the job benefit of taking the MCSE and MCSD exams (which I had prepared for). As an antiquarian predating these things and not really needing them, I saw no point getting them. They are certainly relevant to newcomers and those who depend on a paycheck, and I integrated many of their concepts and even details in this book.

This book serves a double purpose. On one hand it has the practical value for computer programming. On the other it outlines problem solving tools that will help readers understand and apply my later works, some of which are at least as difficult and for which this material is a meaningful prerequisite. I am gravely concerned with technological dependence, the first victims of which are memory, attention (delayed closure), and problem solving. My goal is not to make things difficult, but rather to encourage critical thinking skills that are clearly at risk of extinction. It is my hope that we can tackle the "difficulties" today so future generations are raised with this thinking as second nature. These things are not truly that difficult. Our culture has made them difficult. This has led to a lot of erroneous if not destructive thinking. Science is not about blindly accepting results, yet it is clear that mathematicians and other scientists have no idea how problems are actually solved. If they did, they would question much of what they think they know. This book is as much for them as it is for programmers and project managers.

This edition does not contain the unit-by-unit class project of previous editions, since this publication does not support simultaneous multimedia publication. If you are self-taught, you will do fine if not better creating your own projects. If you are an instructor the projects and data would be useful. Contact me (dobit1969 at yahoo) for electronic copies of classroom materials. I am not generally available for other requests. I no longer take clients and do not guarantee response even to specific questions, especially computer related questions.

# Unit 1—Analyzing Requirements

## Objectives

Dealing with computers only seems difficult. In reality computer problems can always be solved logically. Humans, on the other hand, account for the vast majority of errors and are ultimately the source of problems. Considering the nature of physics, and discounting normal wear and tear, humans are ultimately responsible for all computer problems. Students will understand:

| | |
|---|---|
| 1. Attitude Adjustments (Yours) | 4. Communication Failures |
| 2. Steps to Successful Selling | 5. Overcoming Fear |
| 3. Customer & Manager Perceptions | 6. Analyzing Business Requirements (MCSD) |

## Attitude Adjustments (Yours)

### Failure is...

- A learning experience
- The game played in order to win
- Practice for perfection
- Feedback guiding in new directions
- Opportunity to develop a sense of humor
- Null if you approach all choices with a win-win objective

And finally...The more I fail, the more likely I am to succeed.

### Reasons to do good (what is right)...

The following seem demotivating. On the contrary they must be motivators or you will burn out and wallow in self-pity with false ideas of omnipotence. After the list I have a little story to help you understand these as motivators.

- People are unreasonable, self-centered, illogical, and ignorant (if not completely stupid).
  Love them anyway.
- Although the underdog is favored, people will chum up to the top dog to look good.
  Fight for the underdog
- Honesty and frankness make a person vulnerable.
  Be honest and frank.
- Give your best and you will likely suffer.
  Give your best anyway
- The good done today will be forgotten tomorrow and you will be accused of selfishness.
  Do good anyway.
- What takes years to build can be destroyed in an instant.
  Build anyway.

A thief was staying in a monastery. The monks grew tired of his steeling and went to the master. "If he doesn't go, then we will," they pleaded. "I understand," empathized the master. "It is our duty here to help those whom the rest of society rejects and to guide them toward righteousness. Clearly he needs to remain because he needs guidance. You should go because you do not. The choice is yours." The thief overheard the exchange and never stole again. The reasons listed above assure your work as a professional. When you take them as motivations then they do not become obstacles. With the obstacle removed you can look on others and find their real value, what they have to offer humanity, and respect them. Even if all they have to offer are good intentions. You cannot be disappointed with this view.

## Steps to Successful Selling

Fact: All jobs are sales jobs. You must be able to sell the values and benefits of yourself and the products you have to offer. The following sequential steps are proven effective:

Foreword

Unit 1—Analyzing Requirements

1. Opening (Meet and Greet)—The first 54 seconds of contact establish the entire atmosphere of your communication. You absolutely must make a good first impression with your appearance and verbiage. When you meet someone, welcome them, introduce yourself and get their name. For example, approach the person, shake their hand and say: "Welcome to _____, my name is _____. Your name is...?" The trick is to keep shaking until they give you their name. If it is a group of people, offer your hand to the middle of the group and take the first offering. Do not neglect a single member of the group either. You must greet each one and learn their names. If you are not good with names, get good at talking to people without making it obvious you forgot their name. A handshake should be firm and consistent. If you are answering a phone always identify yourself and your company first, then ask whom you are speaking with. If you are calling them, ask for them by name then identify yourself and your company.

2. Fact-Find—Ask questions leading to discovering the purpose of the visit, what they expect and what they have to offer. For example, "What brings you to _____?" and "How did you learn about us?" This is a continuing process in which you identify their interests and motivations. You can talk about what is of interest to them to pass time during slow moments of the process, which will help build rapport. Remember: **The person asking questions is in control of the communication**.

3. Buy What They Offer—Even if you aren't really buying from them, learn what it is they do, what they have to offer, let them sell themselves and their products and services. This gives them hope for gain, which will encourage them to stick with you.

4. Sell From Stock—Sell what you have, because you do not want to run the risk of selling something else then not being able to provide it. At this stage you guide them through observing your products. Never start with exactly what they are asking. At the least, always step sell them. This means to take them to a lesser product, which you know they will reject. Let them see what it is, how much it is, and what it has to offer knowing they will reject it. When they do then you have prepared them to spend more because it is obvious that their expectations are higher so the price will be also. Through this and the demonstration process pay close attention to body language. Poor negotiators will often let you know blatantly how much they like what you have to offer. A good negotiator will not be obvious.

5. Demo—Demonstrate what you have to offer. This is a very sensitive subject because you can't just go "Here's the product." You must be able to show them the elements of your product in terms they can sense (e.g. the sight, smell, touch and tastes) and how these can be of value or benefit to them. Think of the adage: "Don't sell me bacon, sell me the sizzle and the smell." It can be difficult to get a customer past the demo stage. Many will try to escape even if they really want what is being offered. The most common reason is money. Another common reason is the product is not what they really want. You must smoke out any objections (reasons for not purchasing). What do they like and what do they not like in the product? If necessary show them something else. You would be surprised how many customers come looking for one thing and leave with something completely different. If money is the problem, do not make any promises you cannot keep, but you can say something like "You would purchase this for ___ wouldn't you? Then let's see what we can do." You would also be surprised at how many customers will spend much more than they say they will.

6. Relax—Sit down with them, get them a drink and discuss just about anything other than the product. When you give the customer something then they feel like they owe you something. This allows you to build a little more rapport also before beginning the negotiation process.

7. Write-Up—Begin preparing for the sale by doing any necessary paperwork. This does not mean to stop talking to them. Hand them insensitive documentation to fill out for themselves that only requires listing their personal information. If you deal with credit applications then remember that you must never hand them a credit application to fill out. The credit application does not get filled out at this stage anyway.

8. Call Management—The salesperson's advantage is they are not personally involved with the selling decision. The customer's disadvantage is they are personally involved with the purchase decision. The reason is simple: emotions. Management knows the pricing and what can be done to "make a deal." If you know, then you must put the knowledge aside to ensure you can get the most from the customer. Never rush a sale. When you call management tell them who the customer is and what they wish to purchase. Management must then determine if the product is available. While management is doing

this you explain to the customer that availability is being checked, which gives them fear of loss. Management will then tell you if the item is available, and if it is what it will take to make a deal. Write down the details management gives you about the deal. Note: The phone call is important because you do not want to leave the customer alone. While the manager is checking availability they should be asking you questions, which you relay to your customer, or answer back so the customer understands the questions such as "Did they try what we have to offer?" "Did they like it enough to buy it?" If you are trying to sell yourself and there is no management involved, then this step is replaced with an intermission in which you excuse yourself to consider the offer. Remember that being in demand will help make the sale. Never rush into the decision, but don't make them wait long either.

9. Negotiate Offer—When you hang up the phone turn the paper around which you were writing on. Start with what they have to offer if they are giving you something. Next identify what it is they are purchasing, including its features. Finally tell them the conditions of purchase. Draw an X under the initial sale offer and say, "Please sign here to accept the offer." Shut up! Remember: **The first person who speaks is at a negotiating disadvantage**. If they reject the initial sale offer then ask them what it would take to make the deal. Write down exactly the conditions of their offer. In some industries you will make a second call to management, provide their offer, get a counter offer, show it and explain why then write down their next offer. Have them sign the offer accepted by the customer with a statement to the effect of "I will buy and accept (what they are purchasing) today." Have them write a check or provide some other form of payment or assurance that they are purchasing. They may likely resist. Explain that you will use the surety to convince management their offer is serious, and that without it you will have no negotiating power against management. This keeps you on their side as their advocate in the sale. You must feel like you are their advocate to take this responsibility. If a credit application is required, this is when you fill it out. You must get these three things if you want to make a deal: Cash, Credit Application (if necessary), and Commitment. They are called the 3 Cs. If you cannot get these then I recommend showing them the product again and explaining the values and benefits. Remember: Some industries, particularly with large purchases, require a credit application even if a loan is not involved. The minimum reason is for identification purposes. Before you proceed on to the next step, if they have signed a counter offer then explain that management does not have to accept their offer but that you will do your best. Ask them to wish you luck.

10. Speak to Management—This is when you must leave the customer and meet with management in person. It is purely psychological as is the rest of this process. If you have not succeeded in getting the 3 Cs, then a closer must go in. If a closer comes in, you go with, but you say absolutely nothing unless the closer asks you a direct question. Closing is a fine art discussed below. If a deal is not established, then management must always have the opportunity to talk to the customer before contact is broken. If all goes well, at this stage you finalize the sale.

11. Log Efforts—You must keep track of all sale efforts. Keep detailed records whether they purchased or not. This leads to step 12.

12. Follow-Up—Follow the customer until they die (or ask you to quit following). If the customer is serious about making a purchase, 72% will buy within 48 hours & 92% will buy within 14 days. If you do not follow, then you can rest assured that somebody else makes the sale. If they do purchase, then continue the relationship to be sure of their satisfaction, that they remember you for the next purchase, and they recommend you to others.

### Closing Deals

Closing is essentially reselling, but taking to extremes. The closer will meet and greet and ask the customer about the product they are purchasing and their terms. Where you asked the customer if they liked the product well enough to own it, the closer will treat this differently. Here is an example of a typical close:

| Closer | Customer |
| --- | --- |
| "Did you try our product?" | "Yes." |
| "Did you like it well enough to own it?" | "Yes." If the customer seems at all hesitant, then the closer will go through the Demo step again. |

| "Sorry, I can't sell it to you if you only like it. If you don't love it you will hate whatever I offer within the next 6 months." (This is true!) The closer gets up to leave. | The customer often changes their tone here and becomes an instant buyer. If they don't, the closer must recommend they find something else, even if that means starting over from scratch. |
|---|---|

The closer now has all the advantages. You have spent time wearing the customer down (attrition). The closer has entered, quite often, with absolutely no reference point, so they can start completely fresh. Since the closer is fresh, they do not need to deal with their own emotions. Often by this time the salesperson is also exhausted and having to deal with their own emotions. When you start having to deal with your own emotions you cannot expect to guide someone else's. Without you actually having the sales experience, developing closing skills is nearly impossible.

## Customer & Manager Perceptions

Remember, the customer and your manager are always right until you convince them otherwise. Attacking or putting down their perspective immediately creates barriers and conflict. You never want a conflict with a manager or customer. You will always lose. This does not mean to say Yes when you mean No (see below). Here our concern is gathering information adequately before moving into saying "no" without saying no. That means you must ask questions and effectively listen to what they are telling you. To be certain, rephrase what they have told you and repeat back for clarification. You may need to take notes, and clarification may be best accomplished in writing rather than verbally so you can be sure not to inadvertently sound negative. It is also highly advisable to take this information and put it into practice as you examine other possibilities. Here are some perceptions that can automatically be assumed as incorrect, meaning they must be handled carefully. Never put down a perception. The best approach is to repeat the perception for clarity, than empathize with a statement like "I understand why you would like to have your office automatically perform all its duties when you click one button."

| Perception | Reality |
|---|---|
| I want it all to happen with a single click. | Problem is that you must tell the computer exactly what you want and provide all the necessary information. Whenever possible it is preferred the developer provides the simplest procedures possible, but not for this reason. The simplest procedures reduce human error, which is the real problem. Correct, high-quality work is more important than saving time because poor quality always costs more in the long run. |
| I need a simple change... | If it were simple they would do it themselves. This is potential warning for disaster. Rarely is it as simple as "Bold the title." More likely the simple change involves something like modifying an argument statement to change the output, which could affect more than the desired output. Listen very carefully because you do not want to make a "simple" global change when it should be limited. |
| Why should I upgrade? | If it is not broke, don't fix it! Foreseen breakage is just as good as the real thing. Personally I'd rather foresee breakage and fix it before it affects my data or output. Drastically antiquated systems are bound to break at unexpected times for numerous reasons, and may run dreadfully slow. These reasons alone should justify upgrading, but not necessarily jumping to the top of the market either. Ideally systems should be prepared to be upgraded to help manage the upgrade costs. |
| New/More is better. | More is often less, and new is often filled with bugs. To borrow from Gary Gygax (AD&D), these people can be labeled power users. Power users also like customizing their toolbars and making their system so unique that they are lost going to another. Power using runs up the bills and cuts into productivity. If you do not know what it does, then learn about it before deciding to upgrade into it. Remember also that the box and software have a physical capacity, and that productivity is always slowed to the slowest component. |
| I only have X number of items... | There will always be more. If there was no opportunity for growth, then borrow somebody else's equipment, print masters and photocopy them. Virtually all data is dated and subject to inflation. When data stagnates it loses its usefulness. |
| Instant | Always run parallel systems through the training and troubleshooting process. |

**Yool—4**

| upgrading | Downtime means money. Change must be proven effective before it totally replaces the old. Surprises in IS can be devastating. |
| --- | --- |
| Limit testing | Nothing seems much worse than testing the upgrade on a few of the top users for a couple days. Upgrades must be tested with all denominations of employees in all possible scenarios. You cannot be certain of anything on such a limited sampling |

All these issues must be treated tactfully. Listen, question, repeat, empathize then educate without putting down what exists or is desired. In the end they make the final decision and if they choose incorrectly that is their problem. If you try deciding for them without their permission, then they are likely to go elsewhere to someone who will. They cannot blame you if you follow the steps below.

### Saying "NO" Without Saying No

Nobody likes a "Yes-man" and nobody likes confrontation. Outright saying "no" or putting down someone's ideas or what they have is going to lead to confrontation. The steps in conflict resolution are identified under communication failures. No matter how careful you are there will be times when a conflict emerges, not to mention you are human yourself and it is remarkably easy to slip and inadvertently cause a confrontation. As the provider of a product or service to a customer or manager, you will always lose the confrontation. To avoid confrontations follow these steps (also listed above) in communication:

1. Listen—This means shutting your mouth, maintaining eye contact, hearing and understanding what is being said.
2. Question—If you are to ever interrupt, be sure it is a question to clarify what was just said. If possible listen to everything they have to say then ask your questions and listen attentively to each of their answers before moving to the next question.
3. Repeat—This may be integrated with your questions. It further shows your listening and understanding. I prefer repeating directly, but at times it may be wise to put the repetition into writing. Put it in writing if there can be any doubt as to expectations, priorities, and time frames.
4. Empathize—Show that you understand how they feel, as if you feel it yourself, or have been there before. This is typically not difficult to do as you probably have, unless you have no experience with the product. If you have no experience with the product, then you must be creative and sound like you understand and sympathize.
5. Educate—Remember that you are the expert or they would not need you. You do this every day, or at least much more frequently than they do. Educating someone does not mean you must think of them as stupid. On the contrary they most definitely have experience and skills you do not. They are merely ignorant and it is your responsibility to lift the veil of ignorance by informing them concisely and expertly. You cannot in a brief time tell them everything, nor should you. Educate them enough so they understand the values and benefits of what you are trying to sell.
6. You perform their final decision—This step has some levity depending on the understanding level of the recipient. This levity is based on functionality not on your personal benefit. There are times when you are told to use something that is not appropriate, and the recipient is so clueless that you must disobey to provide the requested results. This falls under Captain Kirk's rules of command, which is seen reflected throughout society. Even our legal system acknowledges that at times laws must be violated to enforce laws. As an example, the Constitution may be violated if and only if there is a compelling interest. The compelling interest test is extremely vague but may be summarized by the utilitarian perspective of "serving the greatest good for the greatest number." In Star Trek, Captain Kirk regularly finds himself in a situation where he must violate the Prime Directive of non-interference with less advanced societies in order to either rescue the society from a natural disaster or to fill the Prime Directive itself. The stories also mention a test which all commanding officers must take before leaving Starfleet Academy called the Kobeyashi Maru. Kirk was noted as being the only cadet to win, but his solution was to reprogram the computer so a solution could arise. Basically this boils down to an attitude: "There is always a way, always alternatives."

The somewhat knowledgeable recipient needs more than flagrant disregard for orders. The reason is they may be able to look at the work and see that you rewrote the rules. If such is the case, the best approach is to provide them with what they ask and alternatives which can then be "sold" as better. If their demand is completely impossible, then it is necessary to show them personally how impossible it is and to show in your references that it is not just a matter of you don't know how.

The fully knowledgeable can be a great resource because they can tell you how to make it work and they have good reasons for doing things the way they do.

The worst scenario to deal with is an indirect order. It is always better to interface with the person who made the decision than a subordinate. Subordinates have no authority to change the decision and cannot be expected to effectively sell a change. Do your best to interface directly with the decision maker. This may mean providing alternatives in a very brief meeting because it was delegated for a reason. If such is not possible you must assume the worst: they know what they are talking about and have their reasons. Reality is they most likely do not know, but it is better to assume the worst than pay the consequences later.

## Communication Failures

| Distractions | Remove all potential distractions. This can perhaps be most difficult in an adult classroom where the students have to attend because their boss said so. Many take this as the opportunity to catch up on gossip. Decrease the distance between you and your audience, turn off fans and other noise sources if necessary, say something condescending toward yourself that is funny, and if necessary recommend people separate and work with others without scolding. For example, "I think you three would do much better closer to the podium so I could help you more." Another technique is to keep talking about the topic (not the distraction) as you approach them, and be sure that you direct everything you say at them. Ask them questions about the topic on hand. Inevitably they will notice they are being singled out. |
|---|---|
| Concision | Get to the point. If somebody wants to go into detailed story telling, let it be the customer. If you are doing extensive story telling, then the customer perceives you wasted their time. If, however, you are the audience to their stories, you are their best friend. That is where you want to be. |
| Motivating | Motivating is a matter of identifying the needs and desires of the individual or group then exploiting those needs and desires. Maslow's Hierarchy of Needs from most important to least are: Physical, Safety, Belongingness, Esteem, Self-Actualization. If you can help fill a need inexpensively you can easily purchase your customer's wallet. |
| Controlling the Conversation | Some individuals are control freaks. They will dominate the communication by talking too much or asking nonsensical questions. Remember the person asking questions is in control, so guide the conversation with questions and repeating back the needs and desires you identify. Those who talk too much need an audience. For such individuals take control by asking closed questions (they require single word answers like yes or no). For those who speak too little, ask more open ended questions then ask even more questions regarding their responses to get the necessary depth. If the customer is paying you by the hour and talks to you the whole time, it is their money, so pay attention and be sure to accomplish something during the conversation. No doubt, they are used to accomplishing dreadfully little in a lot of time, so if you accomplish something they will fill accomplished. |
| General Comprehension | Tech talk and the ability to follow directions are major barriers. With most physical product sales, language is seldom a major issue as the customer has an idea what they are interested in and you can follow their body language. Services, on the other hand, require at least some ability to communicate in a common language. Some individuals are completely incapable of following sequential directions. These individuals need to be provided controlled physical experiences to learn from and the assurance that they cannot do anything any harm. Technical jargon must be avoided unless the customer exhibits a clear understanding. Even then, each time you use a technical term, immediately supply a definition that any human can physically understand. If you can't, then don't use the term. |

| Strong Emotions | All strong emotions are barriers except enthusiasm for what you are talking about. They may have other concerns you must smoke out with questions.  If the concerns may be personal you may pull them aside, tell them what you perceive and ask if there is anything you can do.  If they are angry do not take it personally.  They have probably had the run-around and are mad at the situation in general.  Empathize by listening to their woes and avoiding the pitfalls they encountered previously.  If all else fails, assure them you will get to the bottom of the matter, even if that means taking the problem personally and tracking down the one person on the planet who can solve the problem.  People do not want to get bounced around, and will be immensely happy if you can be the ultimate person to resolve their problem. |
|---|---|
| Negativity (yours) | Use action verbiage like: Right!! Great!! Please follow me... Why would you say that? Wouldn't you agree?  Look at this... Sound good to you?  Let me show you... What I would like to do... I understand, however... |

## Overcoming Objections

Objections are the obstacles between purchasing and not purchasing.  A customer will always buy what they need, so do not count on being able to fill wants too.  The five sequential steps to overcoming objections are:
1.   Smoke out the objection (by asking questions about what is the obstacle and why?)
2.   Identify the objection  (listen to their answers)
3.   Repeat the objection exactly as stated (or at least concisely)
4.   Isolate the object (dissect it into its parts to find the absolute root of the problem and identify the quality you must meet)
5.   Answer the objection (overcome it by meeting the necessary quality or minimizing it)

## Useful Tips

| | |
|---|---|
| • Always assume the sale | • Start transferring mental ownership |
| • Smoke out intentions | • Create desire for ownership |
| • Start building value in your product | • Create a sense of urgency |

In dealing with objections:

| Never | Always |
|---|---|
| Give one objection too much power | Test the validity of the objection |
| Take an objection personally | Remind yourself it is not about you personally |
| Make verbal proposal or solution without writing particulars down | Write down proposed solutions and summarize your efforts in terms of values and benefits |
| Abandon negotiations because of an objection | Use the objection as a focal point for reaching an agreement |
| Confuse the person with the objection | Address the objection without making it about the buyer (e.g. without blame) |
| Let yourself be convinced the objection will prevent the sale | Test the objection for its influence and validity in the process |
| Put the buyer in a non-reversible position (corner them) | Leave it open for the buyer to make a decision ("If you aren't happy then I don't expect you to do business here.") |
| Let objections get your spirit down | Keep your attitude and appearance up (e.g. smile) no matter what |
| Totally ignore an objection | Show empathy and understanding |
| Give in to an objection right away | Check the validity by asking for elaboration |
| Interrupt while they state their objection | Listen and allow them to explain themselves |

Foreword
Unit 1—Analyzing Requirements
### Money Issues

Customers are more resistant to making a decision than parting with money, so eliminate all other objections first. All costs are justified if:
- The customer understands the costs of lesser products
- The customer understands the values and benefits of the product
- The customer perceives good service
- The customer perceives timely professionalism

### Time Issues

Scotty's Law says you should multiply all time estimates by four, then provide the results in half the time. The factor of four guarantees the task is accomplished and is functional without obvious errors. Take twice as long to provide the results as your personal estimate just to be sure it is correct. This also gives you time to run drafts past the customer for approval. Scotty's Law must sometimes be expanded, and most notably with applications development, such as web design, database design, graphics design, etc. Those who have worked in these fields know that most projects can be completed over night.

It is hard to justify charging $30,000 for a database design you did in six hours if the customer knows you took six hours. These projects may be quick for a developer, but you should sit on the project and run test data through it over a period of months before you ask for such a large dollar amount. If they need a quick patch to get by, charge a lot by all means, then take your time delivering the rest. This may seem like a big lie, but in reality there are good reasons for taking your time with development. Often, in primary research, I find it wise to walk away for months or even years, then double back to see if the logic still works and provides the expected results. During the waiting period you must be creative and think about anything that could possibly break the system you devised. You should also think of ways it can be made more concise, or provide extra useful features. DO NOT SHOW A COMPLETE WORKING MODEL UNTIL CLOSE TO THE END OF THE DELIVERY PERIOD! Even then, try to only show parts. It is too easy for the customer to try and rush something that really should be taken slowly and carefully. The more time you have with the development, the less likely it is to break and the more satisfied your customer will be. Instant delivery usually results in thoughts like, "If you could do it that fast, it must be real easy so maybe I should get a book and do it myself." That is not good for business. If they try this, they will be going to someone else to fix what they messed up, and I can almost guarantee they will.

## Overcoming Fear

The largest obstacle between the user and understanding is fear. Fear results from our sense of boundaries, and is useful to our sense of safety. We learn to build boundaries by borrowing those of our elders as we grow up. Boundaries get stronger with age because what could take years to build can be destroyed in seconds, so we get "gun shy." I like to use the following discussion with new users to help destroy their boundaries. Consider the discussion and stories carefully as they may prove helpful. Fear and boundaries are a direct function of age and an inverse function of knowledge. The greater the age, the greater the fear and boundaries. The greater the understanding, the lower the fear and boundaries.

### Elements of Human Nature

The elements of human nature describe not only our purpose here, but the entire nature of Primo Levi's book: The Periodic Table (translated from Il Sistema Periodico). We cannot explore all the elements of human nature, but will place particular emphasis on our sense of boundaries, their source, the ways they create fear in us, and how this affects both learning and interfacing with technology. To accomplish this we will examine two brief stories: Blade Runner (based on the movie by Ridley Scott and the book entitled Do Androids Dream of Electric Sheep? by Phillip K. Dick) and Titanium (from Primo Levi's book The Periodic Table). It is easy to think these stories balance the past with the future, but both have timeless messages regarding human nature that concern us here.

Blade Runner is science fiction that comes close to home not only in dates but also in the current advances and capabilities of technology. Some readers mistakenly are drawn literally into the images based on beliefs and religion without realizing the underlying meanings. The images themselves are easily applied to any religion or conception of human symbolism. Deckard is an anti-hero whose transformation is overcome by what he fears the most: the technology he is intended to destroy. Not only does he find the technology is not to be feared, he discovers himself and inner happiness. There are some factors of the original story omitted from our reading. For example, Rachel is a replicant whom Deckard has innocently fallen in love with before being ordered to destroy her. The movie and book are both overflowing with rich imagery which could not possibly be fit in this short space.

Titanium is an adorable little story until you realize the context in which it is told. Primo Levi survived the Nazi prison camps…. Usually that line is enough to send anyone back to the story because all of a sudden it isn't just a story about a cute, curious little girl and a painter. Suddenly it is a story about the deaths of millions of Jews, Gypsies and homosexuals. Not only is it a story about this, but also of hundreds of millions slaughtered throughout this century in other mass-executions (Mao Tse Tung, Stalin, etc.). This story briefly describes a small area of human nature in which we allow others to construct and destroy our personal boundaries (e.g. values and fears). In the background are countless images alluding to totalitarianism, the number one source of unnecessary mass death: controlling the way other people think. Some of these images include: white (washing: and all from one can everything is painted! e.g. propaganda), paper boat hat (ships were and remain the primary instruments of military power). In spite of all the strange things, Maria trusts the power of the circle. We all do. We all trust the circles constructed for us by those we looked up to as children. That is, until we realize them and our own power to escape and explore on our own.

Why both stories? I have used these stories for several years to teach these same concepts to students in a wide range of fields. Sometimes one story works better than another. Other times both are needed. What determines this is the audience. For this reason the last part of the Windows project is to respond and describe which story best achieves the objectives (overcoming personal fears and boundaries) for you and why. Everyone has fear to one degree or another. Most people have an initial fear of technology because they do not understand. They fear hurting something because their parents always told them "Don't force it! You'll break it!" The most breakable items on a computer are either replaced cheaply or, in the case of software, easily reinstalled. If you lose information, figure out why, go back and make sure it doesn't happen again. When we realize technology is a tool and we are the masters, then we have the courage to make our servant technology work for us.

### Blade Runner

In 1492 a dream began-a dream of prosperity in a far away land, a land we now call America. For many, prosperity meant material wealth and power. It is 2017. Millions scramble and work for the so-called American dream, in the city of the angels: Los Angeles. Monolithic buildings rise above the street markets, a testament to the success of a few overlooking the many, the struggling. Billboards remind the masses that there is a better place, a place off world-and this is a hell to be risen up from. So desperate and wanton of material, of rising up in success, these so-called humans have perfected their art: the creation of cybernetic slaves called replicants. Their motto: to build replicants "more human than human." In their zeal they succeeded.

Realizing their success, they give replicants a shortened life-four years-and a death sentence for acclimating with the "humans" of Earth: issued by bounty hunters called "blade runners." Deckard is a blade runner. He "retires" replicants seeking the ultimate American dream: humanity. Deckard does not like his job-he feels like he is killing "people" not mindless androids. Little does Deckard realize, but his emotion-sense is very accurate. The replicants, in their abbreviated lives, are forced to live, forced to love and appreciate life, where humans take their long lives for granted. The replicants have become more human than the humans.

Today pilgrimages are made to churches, temples and other holy places. The hope: to someday meet the maker-God. Why? To receive eternal life and the answers to the questions: where do I come from? why am I here? where am I going? when? Roy Batty is a religious pilgrim, and his "God," Tyrell, is in Los Angeles. Roy's crime: he is a replicant. Roy is Tyrell's "prodigal son," the embodiment of being "more human than human."

Foreword
Unit 1—Analyzing Requirements

Deckard becomes an unwitting student of Roy's humanity.  Deckard has no aspirations and no faith.  Deckard lives one day at a time, from one bottle of alcohol to the next-knowing no love for himself or anyone else; without compassion.  He drowns the moral dilemma of killing a replicant with liquor, a coward running from his own humanity.  Goff, an omniscient-insightful blade runner, makes a paper chicken (origami) while Deckard searches Leon's apartment.  The chicken represents Deckard's cowardliness.  Later, Goff makes a matchstick man, as with the manikins this symbolizes Deckard's falsity, an empty man, a man without a life nor a soul.

Deckard is asleep at the wheel of life-his eyes do not see.  Roy does see.  He says, "If you could see through your eyes what I can see through mine. . . . "  Roy is a prophet, leading his people to the land of salvation, the promise land, a Messiah of the replicants.  To this end he sacrifices himself and repents: this is Roy's "great moral idea," cementing replicants into a "solid union" of humanity.  He aspires "to eternal aims:" "absolute gladness" in being human.  Roy sees humanity, and repents his birth-sin, being born a replicant, in the image of Christ-driving a nail through his palm.

As the story reaches its climax it is easy to believe that the final conflict is between Deckard and Roy.  Deckard is really confronting himself.  He runs-not from Roy but himself.  Deckard is still a coward, still blind to the reality confronting him, still blind to being human.  Deckard leads an unexamined life-guilty of a wasted life.  Roy, the prophet replicant, is a mirror to Deckard's soul.  Roy does not intend to kill Deckard.  Roy is ultimately human-compassionate enough to give life to the man who has opposed him, killed his friends, killed his lover, who would kill him as well.  Roy seeks forgiveness, with room enough in his heart to forgive Deckard.

As Deckard runs frantically from Roy, he makes a giant leap-a leap for life.  As before, Deckard does not have the strength to complete the leap--Roy does.  As Deckard hangs, clinging to the life he does not have, Roy gives his prophetic hand, raising Deckard from lifelessness.  Roy says, "Quite an experience to live in fear.  That is what it is like to be a slave."  Roy's words are filled with meaning, very deep.  Deckard has been a coward, living in fear of himself.  His fear is like a child's fear of "closet monsters"-absent of realism.  Deckard is a slave to his fear.  Where children fear sleep, fearing the "monsters" will come and devour them, Deckard fears life-being consumed in his own reality.

Roy sets a confused Deckard on the rooftop sanctuary.  Deckard is powerless against Roy's humanity.  Roy knows the value of life-giving it to Deckard.  Roy's final achievement is absolute gladness in death-appreciating his own significance when he says, "All those moments will be lost in time like tears in rain.  Time to die."  Roy got what he came for: a soul.  Roy releases a white dove-a symbol of peace and serenity in the hell where the angels have fallen.  His last moments are harmonious: a poet in words and kind, baring his soul before God and Deckard.  Roy's arms, forming a cross, continue his Christian theme, his messianic character.

Deckard watches with awe as the most human Roy dies.  Deckard has undergone a profound transformation from the esthetical to the ethical.  Only now can Deckard appreciate Goff's words: "It's too bad she won't live . . . but then again, who does?"  Life is precious-not to be wasted in the bottom of a bottle.  He loves life.  He loves himself.  He loves Rachel.  He is no longer a coward-as Goff says, "You've done a man's job sir."  An origami unicorn-the fabled immortal horse who loved nymphs-presents an image of purity, immortality and love.  Everything has been dark, dismal, a hell on Earth.  Now, Deckard is ready for the pure northern lands-a heaven to live and love in.

## *Primo Levi's Titanium*

To Felico Fantino

In the kitchen was a very tall man dressed in a way Maria had never seen.  On his head he wore a boat made out of a newspaper.  As he smoked a pipe, he was painting the pantry white.

It was incomprehensible how all that white could be contained in so small a can.  Maria had a great desire to go over and look inside it.  Every so often the man rested his pipe on the pantry shelf and whistled.  Then he stopped whistling and began singing.  Every so often he took two steps back and closed one eye, or he would go spit in the garbage can and rub his mouth with the back of his hand.  In short, he did so many strange and new things.  It was very interesting to stay and watch him.  When the pantry was white, he picked up the pot and the newspapers up from the floor and carried everything to the cupboard and began to paint that too.

The pantry was so shiny, clean, and white that it was almost irresistible to touch it. Maria went up to the pantry, but the man noticed and said, "Don't touch. You mustn't touch." Maria stopped in amazement and asked, "Why?" "Because you shouldn't," he replied. Maria thought about that, and then asked again, "Why is it so white?" The man also thought for a while, as if the question seemed difficult to him, and then said in a deep voice, "Because it is titanium." The pipe in his mouth made his answer sound like "tee tahl-ee-oh," which Maria interpreted as "ti taglio" meaning "I cut you". Maria felt a delicious shiver of fear run through her, as when in the fairy tale you get to the ogre; so she looked carefully and saw that the man did not have knives either in his hand or near him: but he could have one hidden. Then she asked, "Cut what on me?"-- and at this point he should have replied, "Cut your tongue." Instead, he only said, "I'm not cutting anything: this is titanium."

Maria concluded that he must be a very powerful man. He did not seem to get angry, but was rather good-natured and friendly. Maria asked him, "Mister, what's your name?" He replied, "Felice." He had not taken the pipe from his mouth, so Maria thought he said alice (the i sounds like a long e) meaning small anchoves. And when he spoke his pipe danced up and down but did not fall. Maria stood for a while in silence, looking alternately at the man and the pantry. She was not at all satisfied by his answer and wanted to ask him why he had such a strange name, but then she did not dare because she remembered that children must never ask why. Her friend, a child, was called Alice and it was really strange that a big man should have the same name. But little by little it began to seem natural that he should be called Alice, and in fact she thought he could not have been called anything else.

The painted pantry was so white that comparatively the rest of the kitchen looked yellow and dirty. Maria decided there was nothing wrong in going to look at it up close. Only look, without touching. As she approached on tiptoe an unexpected and terrible thing happened: the man turned and in two steps was beside her. He took a piece of white chalk from his pocket and drew a circle on the floor around Maria. Then he said, "You must stay in there." He struck a match, lit his pipe, making many strange grimaces with his mouth, and then continued painting the cupboard.

Maria sat on her heels and attentively considered the circle for a long time. She became convinced that there was no way out. She tried to rub it at one spot with her finger and saw that the chalk line actually disappeared. She understood very well that the man would not have regarded that system as valid. The circle was evidently magical. Maria sat on the floor quietly, every so often she tried to reach far enough to touch the circle with the tips of her feet and leaned forward so far that she almost lost her balance. She soon realized that there was still a good hand's breadth before she could reach the pantry or wall with her fingers. So she just sat there and watched as gradually the cupboard, chairs, and table also became white and beautiful.

After a very long time the man put down his brush and paint pot and took the newspaper boat off his head. Maria could see he had hair like all other men. Then he went out by the balcony and Maria heard him rummaging around and tramping up and down in the next room. Maria began to call, "Mister!" —first in a low voice, then louder, but not too loud because at the bottom she was afraid that the man might hear.

Finally the man returned to the kitchen. Maria asked, "Mister, can I come out now?" The man looked down at Maria in the circle, laughed loudly, and said many things that were incomprehensible, but he didn't seem angry. At last he said, "Yes, of course, now you can come out." Maria looked at him perplexed and did not move. Then the man picked up a rag and wiped away the circle very carefully, to undo the enchantment. When the circle had disappeared, Maria got up and left, skipping and feeling very happy and satisfied.

## Analyzing Business Requirements (MCSD)

### TCO and ROI

Total Cost of Ownership (TCO) is the overall short and long-term costs of implementing a solution. This not only includes development costs but also the costs of other hardware requirements, corporate infrastructure requirements (the software and everything outside the computer including the office, furniture, cords, hubs, personnel, management and services, etc.) and training. Various models will give or take priority (even eliminating) these items. The objective is not to minimize but to optimize costs. Microsoft's Solutions Framework TCO model views TCO as a continual process with three phases: planning (benchmarks based on industry averages; baselines of actual costs of acquiring, managing and retiring assets; validation and ROI), building (simulated impact on ROI) and managing (validation of TCO optimization strategy against objectives and projections). Short-term savings seldom, if ever, means lower TCO.

The lifecycle approach to TCO optimizes by element: development of code and content, downtime/other for planned and unplanned downtime of development and testing, end-user costs of training and support, hardware and software costs, support of maintenance (disaster recovery, help desk, administration and user training), telecommunications fees for distribution and sharing of information, management of data, networks and systems. Most costs are incurred from the labor of developing, supporting and maintenance. To reduce costs take advantage of existing structures like system policies, logon scripts, and user profiles that require education to overcome. Also, define clearly asset management procedures, standard operating environments, and training. A major objective in TCO planning is to network operations, network and data management, administration and help-desk as self-sufficient as possible to lower user dependence on the IT processes (e.g. users do not have to regularly call the developers to accomplish their tasks).

Return on Investment is a projection estimating how much the client gets financially for the TCO. This might include accounting for increased production, decreased overhead costs, increased reliability of results (e.g. reducing quality control and shrink losses), etc.

## Project Scope

The number and complexity of tasks the project components will perform is the scope. The business process expected to be emulated is the project domain. This must be divided into what will be implemented by humans and what processes will be implemented by your solution, which is your responsibility. The tasks are then divided into modular units. The modularity of your design is then directly affected by the geography of the implementation, the number of expected user, the cost and time limitations of developing. Often the project is bigger than the cost and time limitations permit. The best approach is to present the problem to the client and adjust the scope to meet the restrictions in the meantime. Explain what is being done to accommodate the limitations and what changes are needed to meet the expectations.

## Extent of Requirements

Business requirements are the elements of the project that are required by the client's needs, and are separate from the needs of system requirements (e.g. data access and communications) which are also important to your design. A business requirement is a specific task in the client's workflow. Parts of the task are called business rules, which are written in English then coded to function. Managing inventory is a business requirement, while stating to reorder when the quantity on hand drops below the minimum, is a business rule. Do not confuse business rules with the internal logic of a system, like requiring a keep-alive message be sent to the server when inactivity occurs for a given period of time. Also do not confuse business rules with operating procedures that apply to humans or formatting rules applied to documents. Rules often work together. For example, another rule may specify how an item is reordered.

The extent of requirements is directly affected by the type of problem (communication, messaging, computation, logic, data access, etc.), the required qualities (number of users, maintenance scheduling, unscheduled downtime, etc.), and the quality of the solution. While quality is preferred, no system is perfect (bug-free). As such you must carefully gauge what imperfections are acceptable based on time and cost limitations, and how they are handled. When it comes to cost-effectiveness, businesses do not always chose what is best for them, and more is not always better. The benefits of the system must justify the costs.

## *Security*

In the following considerations and their descriptions I am showing preference for using Active Directory of Windows 2000 as it appears to be the most efficient in defining security systems. The questions of security involve who has access to what information, from where, when and how.

| Consideration | Description |
|---|---|
| Roles | Administrator, Group, Guest, and Client have different degrees of security access. Often administrators have the most and guests have the least, but this is not necessarily correct. It is better to look at roles in terms of groups (e.g. administrators, guests and clients), their roles in the network, and their need for access to parts of the network. |
| Fault Tolerance | This should be approached from a data safety perspective rather than as fault tolerance. Because passwords are fallible (and often shared), different degrees of data safety should be established, then security measures and rules are established based on those levels. |
| Maintainability | Going along with fault tolerance this could include expiration of passwords, validation of passwords as not belonging to a particular language and containing both numbers and text. This category also includes reviewing additions and changes to the system, procedures, physical security of the system, and auditing. |
| Security Database | Stores logon information including logon name, password, and access rights to network resources. It appears the easiest system to manage is Active Directory in Windows 2000, however, for full effect all computers on the network need to have Windows 2000, which may not be cost efficient. Note: Windows 95 and 98 have limited compatibility with Active Directory and NT is completely incompatible. |
| Auditing | This has nothing to do with money. Security audits mean reviewing security procedures, preventing lapses in security, and tracking unauthorized access. |
| Security Levels | Those with the least have access to the least. Start with absolute deprivation of resources then allow access as needed according to grouping of users (see roles). Typically no single individual has total autonomy in all security levels. |
| Existing Methods and Policies | What security levels exist and why? Based on the why you can determine what should be in place, compare that to what exists and recommend additions or changes. |
| Workgroup | The workgroup model stores logon and access information on the individual computers. This is fine for a very small network where there are occasional shared files and folders and network devices (like printers). On a large scale you are better off with a domain architecture using something like Active Directory to manage system resources and centralize the logon and access databases. |

## *Performance*

| Consideration | Description |
|---|---|
| Interoperability | The solution must meet or exceed existing data standards. |
| Response-time | This should be minimized as much as possible, and definitely compared to the existing system, as the client may be justifiably displeased if the new system is slower than the old (unless there was poor quality resulting from the previous system or less features that justify the time loss). |
| Transactions | Number per time slice, bandwidth consumption, and capacity of transactions conducted simultaneously and through time. |
| Barriers | This includes users, infrastructure, computers and other components that may cause bottlenecking resulting in slow or failed performance. |
| Peak vs. Average | It is best to design for functionality during peak usage rather than average. If forced to do average be aware that the system may fail during peak usage. |

## Maintenance

The following considerations should be considered in order

| Consideration | Description |
|---|---|
| Support Staff | You must know the knowledge level and accessibility of support staff (in-house, third party, etc.) for the recipients to determine the necessary resources and training they will need. |
| Distribution Breadth | To whom is the solution distributed and where?  Is support staff available? |
| Recipient Knowledge | While recipient knowledge is important to determine the training requirements, it is not a function of any other part of solution development.  Solution developments must follow organization standards, not be aimed at the lowest common denominator of user. |
| Expectations | What maintenance is expected and who will provide it? |
| Life Cycle | This is a major issue potentially affecting everything.  You need to project into the future.  Assume first there will be no upgrade, and predict how much data will accumulate and the ability of solutions to accommodate.  Then assume that upgrades will occur and determine methods so they can occur. |
| Distribution Method | How will the solution be best distributed? |
| Redistribution | How will you manage reinstallation of applications because files have been corrupted? |

## Scalability and Extensibility

Scalability is the ability of services in the system to run concurrently.  This requires independence of services capable of simultaneous operation on multiple machines.  Extensibility is a function of modularity, allowing services to be individually (asymmetrically) updated (think Component Object Model), meaning the entire system does not need to be rebuilt to make a change.

| Consideration | Description |
|---|---|
| Data Growth | This is a serious issue in database design.  It can be approached in many ways.  You must ask: What data is significant?  For how long?  Does old data get destroyed or archived or a combination of both?  Can it be compressed?  How? |
| Organization Growth | What is the client's projected growth?  This directly impacts audience and data growth. |
| Audience Growth | Will the number of users increase?  Who might they be? |
| Cycle of Use | How long will the solution be used? |

## Availability

| Consideration | Description |
|---|---|
| Operation Times | In systems where there is no time for maintenance, the best solution is to run parallel systems where the clients may be automatically rerouted, then pull one system off-line at a time to perform maintenance. |
| Levels | The number of users who need simultaneous access is calculated based on peak usage. |
| Geography | Distributed applications must provide for networking constraint issues to prevent unnecessary bottlenecking.  This may require replication of components and data.  For example, a quality control system that sends large amounts of data to a network data where housing server could reduce the network bottlenecking (and labor of the data server) by condensing the information and formatting it on the client computer. |
| Downtime | Prepare plans for both scheduled and unscheduled downtimes. |

## *Targeting the Audience*

While it is important to define solutions that are technically feasible, and financially practical and profitable, the solution must be sold to the client (see the first half of this lesson). Individual proposals must each be addressed and diplomatically resolved, politics must be balanced, and communications must be metered based on the client's technical know-how and solution explanations must be thorough in explaining and justifying choices. Other audience targeting concerns follow.

| Consideration | Description |
|---|---|
| Environment | Account for the physical environment needs of the computer. |
| Accessibility | Account for the proximity of the user to the computer versus the amount and method of use. |
| Special Needs | Account for the physical limitations of the user based on handicaps, context of use, and other special input methods. |
| Users | Account for the capabilities of the users, including linguistic, cultural, experience level, training requirements and working conditions. Account for outside access to or portability of resources if necessary to accommodate roaming users. |
| Support/Help | Account for technical support for the users and administrators, including any necessary training and documentation. |

## *Integrating with Existing Systems*

| Issue | Description |
|---|---|
| Legacy application compatibility | Do not attempt to completely redefine everything and deprive the client of existing structures they are familiar with (their comfort zone). It is wise to initially maintain legacy software until the new software is comfortable with the users. As such the new system must be compatible with the old (e.g. get data from it and send data to it). This does not mean you cannot give new features, because those are likely the whole reason you developed a new solution, and will eventually mean all users convert to the new. |
| Connectivity to existing applications | Be cautious of replacing other existing systems just to make the new one work. For example, you introduce a new database system with Access, with procedures that require users to use Excel instead of the existing Lotus 1-2-3 unless you can really justify the change. You want the new system to integrate with old systems as much as possible. |
| Format and location of existing data | Prepare for data transfers by identifying its format, how it will be transported, from where to where. |
| Data conversion | To optimize connectivity to legacy and existing applications you need to account for conversion methods, either in code as an utility or less preferably through procedure. You cannot expect perfect convertibility with all other applications, so I recommend at least providing conversion to the most common and simplest formats. |
| Data enhancement | This may include new formatting methods, data compression, or simply new data. Each of these will pose problems with compatibility. A certain obstacle to compatibility is changing data types and shapes. |

## *Business Methods and Limitations*

| Consideration | Description |
|---|---|
| EDI | Electronic Data Interchange is used for batch transferring of information between banks and between businesses. On the Internet, ASP and CGI are used as a form of EDI available to individuals also. According to the Electronic Commerce Innovation Centre: "The transfer of structured data, by agreed message standards, from one computer to another, by electronic means." Communicating systems are synchronized by sequencing and formatting data at the presentation level of the |

| | OSI. |
|---|---|
| Business Practices | Ideally meet current practices, and only if absolutely necessary propose modifying those practices. |
| Needs | Sometimes the most difficult thing to identify, as often the client believes the problem is in one place and the solution is several places removed. You must be able to smoke out the needs by examining the whole process to find faults, bottlenecks, points that can or must be changed, etc. |
| Organization Structure | This includes both business politics and workflow. |
| Budget | If the solution exceeds the budget constraints seek a lesser solution and present the issue to the client. |
| Deployment | Distributing, implementing and training may be affected by existing systems. The schedule must accommodate for full functionality of the new system, or full functionality of incremental parts. |
| Quality Control | Aim for optimum in your solution and work with the client's QC department to ensure you meet or exceed their requirements and documentation therefore. |
| Process Engineering | Attempt to follow or at least understand their methods for developing solutions. |
| Legal Issues | While these should be left ideally to the client's lawyers, you need to be aware of legal issues surrounding your solutions, not limited to liability, copyright, privacy and libel conflicts. |
| Acceptance | There is always resistance to change, and the more extreme the change the greater the resistance. Always account for the degree of technical complexity the client is willing to accept. The simplest solution that also meets requirements is always the best. Reluctance comes from: fear of extensive additional work, fear of inability to interface with the new system, fear of unfamiliarity/dissatisfaction of abandoning the familiar, fear jobs are being challenged, and fear of obsolescence/downsizing. |
| Computer Environment | Hardware and software (operating system) platforms, and the abilities of the client's technical staff are serious issues of your solution. Try to retain and utilize as much of the existing system as possible, and thoroughly justify any alteration or addition. |
| Migration | Migrating to the new system requires careful planning and consideration of: impact on production, testing, post migration interruptions, and contingency planning for possible conflicts and failures. |
| Infrastructure | The total set of resources necessary to implement and support an enterprise's computing environment. This includes technologies and standards, operational processes (policies, procedures, services), people/staff and organizational skills (e.g. knowledge and management). The military uses Logistics in a similar manner. |

# Worksheet 1—Analyzing Requirements

## Part 1—Sales

Identify by name the twelve steps of selling in order and define them conceptually.

1. _____ _____

   _____

   _____

2. _____ _____

   _____

   _____

3. _____ _____

   _____

   _____

4. _____ _____

   _____

   _____

5. _____ _____

   _____

   _____

6. _____ _____

   _____

   _____

7. _____ _____

   _____

   _____

8. _____ _____

_____

_____

9. _____ _____

_____

_____

10. _____ _____

_____

_____

11. _____ _____

_____

_____

12. _____ _____

_____

## Part 2—Objections

Identify by name the five steps to overcoming objections in order and define them conceptually.

13. _____ _____

_____

_____

14. _____ _____

_____

_____

15. _____ _____

_____

16. _____ _____

_____

_____

_____

17. _____ _____

_____

_____

## Part 3—Analyzing Business Requirements

| Security | |
|---|---|
| a. Auditing<br>b. Fault Tolerance<br>c. Maintainability<br>d. Roles<br>e. Security Database<br>f. Security Levels<br>g. Workgroup | 18. The different degrees Administrators, Groups, Guests, and Clients have<br>19. From a data safety perspective: established degrees of data safety, security measures, and rules are established based on those levels.<br>20. Includes expiration of passwords, validation of passwords as not belonging to a particular language, and containing both numbers and text. This category also includes reviewing additions and changes to the system, procedures, physical security of the system, and auditing.<br>21. Stores logon information including logon name, password, and access rights to network resources.<br>22. Reviewing security procedures, preventing lapses in security, and tracking unauthorized access.<br>23. Those with the least have access to the least. Start with absolute deprivation of resources then allow access as needed according to grouping of users.<br>24. Logon and access information stored on the individual computers. |
| **Performance** | |
| a. Interoperability<br>b. Response-time<br>c. Transactions<br>d. Barriers<br>e. Peak vs. Average | 25. It is best to design for functionality during peak usage rather than average. If forced to do average be aware that the system may fail during peak usage.<br>26. Number per time slice, bandwidth consumption, and capacity of transactions conducted simultaneously and through time.<br>27. The solution must meet or exceed existing data standards.<br>28. This includes users, infrastructure, computers and other components that may cause bottlenecking resulting in slow or failed performance.<br>29. This should be minimized as much as possible. |
| **Maintenance** | |
| a. Distribution Breadth<br>b. Distribution Method<br>c. Expectations<br>d. Life Cycle<br>e. Recipient Knowledge<br>f. Redistribution<br>g. Support Staff | 30. Assume first there will be no upgrade, and predict how much data will accumulate and the ability of solutions to accommodate. Then assume that upgrades will occur and determine methods so they can occur.<br>31. Do not aim for the lowest common denominator of user.<br>32. How will the solution be best distributed?<br>33. How will you manage reinstallation of applications because files have been corrupted?<br>34. To whom is the solution distributed and where?<br>35. What maintenance is expected and who will provide it?<br>36. You must know the knowledge level of these to determine the necessary resources and training they will need. |

| Methods and Limitations | |
|---|---|
| a. Acceptance<br>b. Computer Environment<br>c. Deployment<br>d. EDI<br>e. Infrastructure<br>f. Legacy Equipment<br>g. Migration<br>h. Needs<br>i. Organization Structure<br>j. Process Engineering | 37. Always account for the degree of technical complexity the client is willing to accept.<br>38. Antiquated hardware and software that must be accommodated for.<br>39. Attempt to follow or at least understand their methods for developing solutions.<br>40. Careful planning and consideration of: impact on production, testing, interruptions, and contingency planning for possible conflicts and failures.<br>41. Distributing, implementing and training may be affected by existing systems. The schedule must accommodate for full functionality of the new system, or full functionality of incremental parts.<br>42. Electronic Data Interchange is used for batch transferring of information between banks and between businesses.<br>43. Hardware and software (operating system) platforms, and the abilities of the client's technical staff are serious issues of your solution.<br>44. The total set of resources necessary to implement and support an enterprise's computing environment. This includes technologies and standards, operational processes (policies, procedures, services), people/staff and organizational skills (e.g. knowledge and management). The military uses Logistics in a similar manner.<br>45. This includes both business politics and workflow.<br>46. To identify, examine the whole process to find faults, bottlenecks, points that can or must be changed, etc. |
| **Scalability and Extensibility** | |
| a. Audience Growth<br>b. Cycle of Use<br>c. Data Growth<br>d. Organization Growth | 47. How long will the solution be used?<br>48. What data is significant? For how long? Does old data get destroyed or archived or a combination of both? Can it be compressed? How?<br>49. What is the client's projected growth?<br>50. Will the number of users increase? Who might they be? |

# Unit 2—Hardware & Software

## Contents

### Lesson 1—Computers

| | |
|---|---|
| 1. Computers in General<br>2. Computer Types | 3. System Unit Components<br>4. Motherboard Components |

### Lesson 2—Hardware

| | |
|---|---|
| 1. CPU (Central Processing Unit)<br>2. Other Major Computer Chips<br>3. Secondary Storage | 4. Input and Output<br>5. Expansion and Peripheral System Components |

### Lesson 3—Software

| | |
|---|---|
| 1. Operating Systems | 2. Major Software Types |

### Lesson 4—Purchasing a Computer

| | |
|---|---|
| 1. System Source<br>2. CPU | 3. Expandability<br>4. Peripherals<br>5. Software |

# Lesson 1—COMPUTERS

## Objectives

| | | | |
|---|---|---|---|
| 1. | Computers in General | 3. | System Unit Components |
| 2. | Computer Types | 4. | Motherboard Components |

## Computers in General

### Data Types

Data types are typically divided into text, graphics, audio and video, but would include other forms of output when robotics is involved or other physical operations like printing. Data is stored using binary codes (on/off or 1/0 switches) called bits in bundles called bytes. The smallest byte consists of eight bits. All bytes and storage capacities are divisible by eight. Windows 95 uses a 16-bit bundle per byte, while Windows 98 uses a 32-bit bundle per byte. The advantage of large byte bundles is the ability to store a wider variety of information in greater detail in less space (e.g. graphics). The computer only understands binary bundles, so all information given to the computer is converted into binary, and all output must be interpreted from binary to provide useful information to the user.

### Storage

Primary (internal) storage (memory) temporarily holds information (input, software, and output), while secondary (external) storage stores the information for later sessions of use. Secondary storage is typically built into systems (e.g. the disk drives). The primary storage in a computer is the RAM. When the computer does not have enough RAM to store all the information being processes, Windows 95 and above will create swap files, which are temporary files, on the hard drive to make up for the deficiency.
As we discussed previously, data is stored in binary. Both primary and secondary storage are measured in the number of bytes they can contain. A kilobyte (Kb) is one thousand bytes (more accurately 1,024 bytes) of information. A megabyte (Mb) is a million bytes (more accurately, 1,024,000) bytes of information. A gigabyte (Gb) is a billion bytes of information. As you may have noted, the actual quantities are slightly higher. The reason is these are also divisible by eight.
Conventional RAM ranges from 32 Mb (minimum) to 258 Mb and beyond. Although 32 Mb is adequate, 64 Mb is practical for most general use. Typically more RAM is not necessary unless the computer is used for heavy graphics or otherwise is expected to process extremely large amounts of information. AltaVista's on-line computers, for example, run several Gb of RAM to support their enormous database. Computer purchasers should also be attentive to Shared RAM. Some computers will designate some of the RAM to video and audio, hence sharing the RAM. Others will use accelerator cards with their own built-in memory, which should be preferred but is not necessary unless you expect to do a lot of graphics, video games or otherwise process large amounts of data. There are a variety of RAM types, most popular of which at present is PC100. The type specifies the type of BUS (see Motherboard Components below) necessary to attach the RAM board to the motherboard. In the case of PC100, the 100 refers to the speed of the memory in megahertz (100 MHz).
Secondary storage devices have a wide range of storage sizes. 3.5" floppies store from 720 Kb (for DD) to 1.44 (for HD). CD ROMs store 640 Mb (CD-RWs store up to 720 Mb). Hard (fixed) disk drives currently range from 3.2 Gb to over 80 Gb. The typical user will not currently need more than 6.4 Gb on a hard drive.

### Hardware versus Software

Hardware is the physical equipment, while software consists of the commands that makes the equipment perform actions. Hardware consists of two major categories: the system unit and peripherals. The system unit is the computer case and everything inside the computer case. The actual computer is the CPU (discussed later), while everything not in the CPU (including the motherboard) is considered external to the

Lesson 1—COMPUTERS
Unit 2—Hardware & Software

computer, even if it is inside (internal to) the system unit.  Peripherals are everything that is plugged into
and is external to the system unit (e.g. mouse, keyboard, printer, monitor, scanner, etc.)
A program is a set of instructions that tells the computer what actions to perform and how to perform them.
Applications software perform tasks involving user input and outputting information in a useful format for the
user.  System software enables applications software to run on the system's hardware devices, also called
the Operating System.

## Computer Types

### General Use Microcomputers

Devices using microprocessor technology that perform computations built into other devices such as
calculators, clocks, stereos, microwave ovens, cars, etc.

### Microcomputers (PCs)

Computers constructed using microprocessor technology small enough for common availability and use.
Sizes range from palmtop (handheld) to desktop.  PC and Mac are hardware platforms whose components
are typically incompatible and require different programs to operate.

### Midrange Computers

Also called minicomputers, are often used as servers for networks with too many users to fit the capabilities
of a PC.  These systems may range from the size of a desktop to the size of a desk or large filing cabinet.

### Mainframes

A large computer, typically filling a room, used in large organizations with large amounts of data and many
network users.  These handle high volume jobs, such as billing for a large company.

### Super Computers

Typically not as large as mainframes, but considerably more powerful as they are capable of performing
extensive computations with extreme accuracy.  These are often used in scientific applications and
computer animation for movies.

## System Unit Components

| Casing/Housing | The box that contains the computer's internal components.  Not any box will do, as boxes are designed for specific boards, power supplies, etc. |
|---|---|
| Controller Cards (Add-In Boards) | These are also called **expansion** cards.  This will include cards for controlling external devices, accelerator cards, drive controller cards, most modems and network cards, etc. |
| Drives | Although drives are technically external storage devices, typically at least one floppy drive, a fixed drive and CD ROM drive are built into the box. |
| Peripheral/External Devices | This includes all the input and output devices: monitors, keyboards, pointing devices, printers, etc.  These are not part of the CPU but are attached to it. |
| Motherboard | A large printed circuit board (PC board) intimately connected with all the computer components.  The components of the Motherboard are listed below. |
| Power Supply | Regulates and distributes electricity to the components of the computer.  On examination you will note that one set of cables goes to the Motherboard.  Other cables also go to the drives as a minor indication that they are separate from (and external to) the primary computer unit (the Motherboard and the controller cards). |
| System Fan | Attached to the hottest part of the computer (the Power Supply).  The fan pulls air through little vents around the computer (usually opposite of the power supply so air passes over the Motherboard), and blows the air out the back of the Power Supply.  In |

old systems this was the only item to control the temperature in the computer.

## Motherboard Components

The motherboard is a printed circuit board holding most, if not all of the major computer chips, but always the Processor (CPU). Other components of the motherboard include:

| | |
|---|---|
| Battery | The system battery maintains the system clock while there is no external power to the system. Old batteries were long thin rectangles. Newer models use a large round battery. |
| BIOS | See CMOS below. Basic Input/Output System: The BIOS designates your boot sequence (the order in which the computer checks the drives for the system files to start the computer) and other primary settings of your computer. It may be modified by booting the computer and pressing the [Delete] button on your keyboard when prompted to do so (about the same time the computer is checking its memory). In later Pentiums you can boot off of the CD-ROM, which is useful for Windows 98 and Linux installations. Note: some BIOS features include a virus protection feature that will halt the system if anything attempts to write to the boot sector or partition table of the hard disk during the boot sequence. |
| BUS | Slots into which expansion boards may be inserted, to include AGP for video cards, ISA and PCI for most expansion boards, and DIMM for RAM (e.g. EDO and SDRAM (includes PC100)). BUS speed, measured in megahertz (MHz) affects the rate at which information is transferred from one board to another. The current standard is 100 MHz, though some are slower and current technology makes 200 MHz possible. |
| CMOS | Set of instructions providing the basic interface between hardware devices and the operating system stored on an EPROM (erasable/programmable read-only memory) chip. Sets the current date and time, the type of hard and floppy disk drives installed, and the display type. The BIOS typically auto-detects the memory size. From the CMOS you can access the BIOS features setup where you can enable and disable components, set the boot sequence, set a system password, etc. |
| Co-Processors | Other processor chips apart from but contributory toward the function of the CPU, such as a math co-processor. |
| CPU | See next lesson. |
| Jumpers and Switches | Jumpers and switches are physical components that must be manually set before the motherboard is used. Jumpers, unless otherwise specified here, are used to: identify the processor, set the processor voltage (switches), use a number 2 key on the keyboard to turn the system power on, select the DIMM clock, temporarily clear the CMOS, set the Network Interface Card (NIC) to wake the system (Wake On LAN or WOL), and to set a Sound Blaster (SB) LINK. |
| Ports | Many motherboards have connectors built into them for the mouse, keyboard and monitor. Any socket a peripheral device may be plugged into is called a port. Ports come in two types: LPT (for printers, scanners and other stand alone (e.g. also plug into the wall) devices ), COM (for communications devices, mice, keyboards and other dependent peripherals) and USB (optional in later Pentiums) for high speed connections to components that would otherwise plug into either LPT or COM (MACs alone support USB mice). |
| Processor Fan | A powerful fan mounted directly on top of the processor. This fan forces air very rapidly over the processor, keeping the processor the coldest part of the computer. |
| Slots (IDE & ESDI) | These slots specifically connect to the drives using a wide ribbon to reduce cross-talk (information jumping from one line to another) and increase communications speed (up to 10 million bits per second or Mbps). |

# Lesson 2—HARDWARE

## Objectives

| | |
|---|---|
| 1. CPU (Central Processing Unit) | 4. Input and Output |
| 2. Other Major Computer Chips | 5. Expansion and Peripheral System Components |
| 3. Secondary Storage | |

## CPU (Central Processing Unit)

### Processors in General

The CPU is the central processing unit, which performs arithmetic operations and controls the flow of information among the hardware components. The CPU is composed of an arithmetic/logic unit (ALU), control unit (which directs the flow of electronic traffic), registers (storage area for processing ALU and control unit operations), and buses (the parts connecting the CPU to the motherboard and its components). CPU is also often used as a general term for the main computer unit (the box with motherboard, memory, etc.). The CPU speed is measured in megahertz (MHz), which indicates the chip's rate of performing calculations in processing commands.

The processor contains one or more control units depending on the type of processor. Here we will use the Intel names generically to apply to all equivalent chips. As we progress from lesser to greater processors we should note that later processors contain the control units of the lesser processors. Typically these are improved upon as more is added to the chip. The original PC processors (8086 through 80386) contained only a logic unit. Each had a different footprint (the layout of pins attaching the chip to the motherboard) and different speeds. The 8086 and 8088 (processor on laptops) contained the logic unit to process commands and the BIOS supported 5¼ floppies. The 80286 BIOS supported low density 3½ and high density 5¼ floppies. The 80386 BIOS was capable of supporting the high density 3½ floppies and an arithmetic expansion card. The 486 added internal modems to the list of capabilities and put the arithmetic unit onto the processor. The cache was an innovation of Pentium II chips. The advantage of the cache is that the processor is not waiting on BUS speeds (60MHz on Celeron and under, 100MHz on PII and higher, 200MHz on AMD K7) to retrieve commands to process. Cache is memory directly connected to the processor itself and not the motherboard (most Celerons 128k, PII and some Celerons 256k, PIII 512k, AMD K7 Athelon 8,192k). The illustration shows the basic makeup of processors in the range of Celeron through AMD K7 (simply remove components from the diagram for the lesser processors as indicated above).

### Pentium Processors

All computers with Pentium or equivalent processors are multimedia machines. This is a product of the system board and not the processor chips themselves. These system boards automatically support CD ROM's, speakers and microphones. You can configure the BIOS to place the CD ROM in the boot sequence (Linux and Windows 98 provide bootable CD ROM's and you can make bootable CD ROM's with a CD ROM burner). The only significant differences between the 486 and original 586 processors is the footprint, speed, and multimedia capabilities of the system (mother) board. Celeron and greater computers also provide USB high-speed connections (for some cameras, printers and scanners) and MIDI ports (for joysticks, music keyboards, and some cameras).

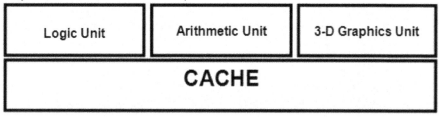

*Cache*

Later Pentium quality chips contain potentially two levels of cache. Level 1 cache is integrated circuit in the CPU. Level 2 cache is on a printed circuit board attached directly onto the CPU. Information travels fastest within an integrated circuit (IC), then second fastest over a printed circuit (PC board), third by ribbon cable to the IDE on the motherboard, fourth by BUS (which connects two printed circuit boards), and slowest by cable. The advantage of cache is a reduction of processing time by reducing the necessity to go through the motherboard, memory BUS, and memory board to the memory (RAM) chip to get the next command. The less frequently this has to occur, the faster the processor can work. A misleading point of processors is their clock speed. While they may clock at a very high speed they may actually run slow because they are waiting to retrieve the next commands. Hence the cache and BUS speeds are extremely important in accelerating operations. The AMD K3 and Athelon chips both have Level 1 cache (128k and 512k respectively). Naturally their processors are the fastest on the current market. Both however are slowed to the lesser components, and at the time of this writing, nothing is actually built to support the 200 MHz BUS speed capabilities of the Athelon, which is disappointing.

## Other Major Computer Chips

Internal memory comes in two forms: RAM (Random Access Memory) and ROM (Read Only Memory). RAM is used for the temporary storage of information, such as commands and data, and may be considered the working memory. RAM is written to and read from throughout the processes of the computer, starting as empty when the computer is started. ROM is used for permanent storage of information that cannot be written to by the user. Typically hardware components contain one form of ROM or another that contains information that allows the hardware to be operated by the rest of the system (makes it compatible). These forms may include a ROM chip, hardwiring, switches, or other parts that a physically manipulable. In General Use Microcomputers the ROM often stores the programming necessary to perform the functions. In old computers, such as Commodore computers, the ROM contains an interpreter to convert program instructions telling the computer what to do into useful commands telling the computer how to perform the action.

| RAM | Random Access Memory. This is the working memory of your computer, where your work and the programs you are running are stored while you are using them. |
|---|---|
| ROM | Read Only Memory means what it sounds. Though information be retrieved and used, it cannot be altered. Old computers used ROM as a place to store the operating system. You would write a program in the OS language (BASIC for example), and the ROM would be used to convert your program into something recognizable and usable by the bios. |
| Virtual RAM | This is a section of your hard disk set aside by Windows to be used as RAM. Virtual RAM is regulated by the operating system (a.k.a. Paging File in Windows 2000). |
| Video RAM | RAM set aside specifically for the purpose of speeding up your video interface. There is also audio RAM on some accelerators specifically for speeding up sounds. |

## Secondary Storage

This refers to components that provide permanent or semi-permanent storage of information, such as the full variety of drives (tape, CD, floppy, hard or fixed, zip, etc.). A drive is a piece of equipment classified as a storage device that reads from and usually writes to a storage unit.

Storage units are classifiable in many ways, many of which overlap. Storage units may come in the form of tapes or disks; fixed or removable; read-only, writable, or rewritable; magnetic, optical (CD) or paper (e.g. teletype tape).

Magnetic disks are rewritable and may be either removable or fixed. Most require formatting before use, which defines the way information is stored onto the disk in what are called clusters (large bundles of bytes). Clusters are bundled into a larger group called a sector. The information is actually stored on tracks in binary form, just as a phonograph record stores sound. A "hard disk" or "fixed disk" is a high-density physical disk or group of disks within a hard disk drive. These are typically the largest of the class of magnetic disks, and typically central to the operations of the computer. The computer uses this disk to store the operating system, program files, and user-generated files. The only way to remove this disk is to remove the drive itself. Floppy disks come in a variety of sizes and two fundamental shapes. They are removable by the user with the simple push of a button or the turning of a knob on the front of the computer. Both floppy and fixed disks require formatting, and may be formatted with a boot sector in which an operating system is placed. The boot sector always occupies the same portion of a disk. This portion of the disk also provides the formatting information about the disk and is a common place for viruses to be stored.

| Drives Always Present | Fixed/Hard | Other Drives Available (common) | 5¼" Floppy Drive |
|---|---|---|---|
| | Floppy (3½") | | SuperDisk (3½" 120 MB) |
| | CD ROM (read-only in all multimedia computers) | | Readable/Writable CD ROM (CD-R) |
| | | | Readable/Rewritable CD ROM (CD-RW) |
| | | | Zip Drive |
| | | | Tape Drive |

## Input and Output

Input is the information provided by the user, provided electronically through the input devices, or taken from previous input or output in secondary storage. All data on the computer was, at one time, either manually inputted or generated by computer processes of manually inputted data. Both qualify as input. Output is the useful information generated by the computer in one of the data forms. To receive output, the user must perform an action, which is perceived by the computer and then processed. This action may be as subtle as turning on the computer (e.g. the boot sequence) or as obvious as keying information into a file that is processed by a program.

## Expansion and Peripheral Components

| Communications Devices | Input Devices | Pointing Devices |
|---|---|---|
| Modem (Analog) | Keyboard | Joy Stick |
| ISDN Modem (Digital) | Mouse | Light Pen |
| Satellite Receiver | Trackball | Mouse |
| Networking Card | Touch Pad | Track Balls |
| Laser/Light Communications | Other Reverse Pointers | Reverse Mice/Pointers: |
| | Light Pen | Thumbelina |
| **Output Devices** | Scanners | Touchpad |
| Monitor (CRT) | Digital Camera | Thumb knob/pointer |
| Printer | Microphone | |
| Other Monitors | | |
| Speaker | | |

# Lesson 3—SOFTWARE

## Objectives

Students will understand:

| 1. Operating Systems | 2. Major Software Types |
|---|---|

## Operating Systems

Each hardware component uses different machine language instructions to operate. Drivers are used to tell the operating system how to communicate with the components. The operating system balances the communications between the user and the software (the user interface) and between the software and available hardware components. The operating system defines how information is stored, where it is stored and how it is processed. The operating system also provides common routines that are used by all programs (e.g. the Open and Save As dialog boxes, all title bar and most dialog box components, etc.) Windows 95 is the first Windows version to be an operating system for IBM's. Before Windows 95, PCs used DOS (Disk Operating System) which is a textual user interface. Windows was run as an application on top of DOS, which significantly slowed the system. The first popular Windows version was 3.1. By the time Windows 95 arrived as a combined graphical user interface (GUI pronounced goo-ee) and operating system, the MAC OS (also a GUI) had been used nearly a decade. As a consequence, MAC cornered the market in publishing and graphics design in the mid-80s, where it is now losing ground to less expensive, and significantly more popular PCs. By integrating windows and the operating system, programs can run faster. Versions A and B of Windows 95 used a 16 bit system to accommodate their use of graphics. Version C of Windows 95 introduced the 32-bit system to accommodate more colors. With 32 bits, a larger amount of data can be compressed more meaningfully in a smaller space. Windows 98 introduced a 32-bit File Allocation Table (FAT 32). Previously information was stored in 32 bit clusters (two bytes per cluster). The FAT 32 uses 4 bit clusters so files can be compressed much smaller (black and white line art only needs four bits). FAT 32 also reduces the need for partitioning larger drives. Equipment is already available to handle 64 bit processing, which will significantly improve 3-D graphics.

## Major Software Types

- Word Processing—These are programs that you may enter text and graphics into, lay out pages and generally create most documents.
- Desktop Publishing—Specialized programming that produces professional documents, such as card layouts, labels, etc. Desktop Publishing is generally surpassed by the superior quality of the program more commonly viewed as a word processor known as Microsoft Word.
- Spreadsheets—Create documents divided into rows and columns, in which formulas may be used to link data, calculate, analyze and graph within the same worksheet.
- Databases—Create electronic filing cabinets of information, which can be cross-referenced, searched, analyzed, reported from, etc.
- Presentation—Provide a means for integrating a computer-based presentation using slides of text and graphics.
- Communications and Browsers—This would include dialup networking (Windows 3.11 and better). These programs allow computers to communicate with each other remotely. Browsers recognize only certain program types allowing unlike machines to communicate over a wide area. We will discuss browsers in greater detail in our next unit.
- LAN vs. WAN—Local Area Networks connect computers within immediate proximity, such as within an office. A network between computers in separate buildings may be a LAN if they are connected by an internal means (e.g. not by telephone but by cable, microwave, etc.). Wide Area Networks are broader and may include LANs. These are remote networks where computers communicate with each other by telephone, such as the Internet. Some LANs are considered WANs by their administrators simply because the computers are not directly hard-wired to each other (such as using Satellite or Microwave

communications equipment). Often WANs are set up to limit the impact of individual users on the server. Users may request information but may not be able to add or change information. LANs come in multiple forms, but the primary distinction lay in dumb-terminal and peer networks. Peer networks are composed of separate computers that do not require the server to function, but will share information with the server and other peer workstations. Dumb terminals run programs, retrieve and store information directly with a server.

- E-mail Software—Manages incoming and outgoing electronic mail. Typically these allow you to read, write, respond to, and archive messages, and to save attached files to a specified drive.
- Personal Information Management Software—Similar to project management except that typically this will include address books, personal scheduling, etc. without in-depth analysis. Many of these allow multiple users.
- Personal Finance Software—helps track income, expenses, pay bills, conduct transactions and evaluate personal financial plans. This would not be a program you could run payroll through as it would not provide the programming for deductions, calculating earnings from hours and pay rate, etc. as an accounting program would. It also lacks in the reporting capabilities of a complete accounting program.
- Project Management—Provides scheduling, tracking and analysis of resources, events, costs, etc. associated with a project. Typically this means you can maintain multiple projects under different names, and retain a record of them, which is helpful if you are forced to make detailed reports of your projects and/or must work or supervise multiple projects simultaneously.
- Accounting—Goes beyond personal finance to include accounts receivable and payable, invoicing, inventory, etc. One of the benefits of these programs is they update to match current tax requirements, including creating essential tax reports. Of course these updates must either be purchased or subscribed to, and typically a subscription comes with the program so the user is current. A good example of this is PeachTree.
- Groupware—A collaborative program that allows multiple users to access and alter information in a network environment, or as multiple users of the same computer. MS Office has this feature as well, allowing documents to be secured by password and user name, and thereby to allow embedding of the author name, date and time of modification, etc.
- CAD—Computer Aided Design typically enables three-dimensional design in-scale, including the ability to rotate, zoom, templates, etc. Some only work in two dimensions, which can also be accomplished with many graphics programs like PhotoPaint.
- Multimedia Authoring Software—allows you to create presentations that include text, graphics, sound, animation and video.
- Integrated and Software Suites—Common examples include packages containing a word processor, database and spreadsheet (MS Office, Works, Claris Works). Corel also provides one that comes with Object Character Recognition (OCR), PhotoPaint, Ventura Publishing.
- Object Linking and Embedding—Linking relates data between documents or compounded between documents of separate programs, requiring both to be open simultaneously, so changes affect both together. Embedding allows you to make changes in destination documents without altering the source document.

# Lesson 4—PURCHASING A COMPUTER

## Objectives

Students will understand the basic principles involved with making a purchase decision to include:

| | | | |
|---|---|---|---|
| 1. | System Source | 3. | Peripherals |
| 2. | Expandability | 4. | Software |

## System Source

The source of your system is extremely important. It is wise to stick to major name brands and to talk to a technician about which brands are most reliable. Prices of personal computers make building your own not cost effective unless you are building a high-end server and really know what you are doing. Be skeptical of purchasing from any manufacturer who uses substandard components.

### MAC or PC?

Although Macintosh provided the first graphic user interface, their systems are waning in flexibility, expandability and costs. As a rule of thumb, be sure whatever you buy (software and hardware) is compatible with your work and school needs (what they have). Macintosh is a likely candidate when working with the publishing, graphics design or music industries. Some schools still use Macintosh. In any of these cases, verify the need before making your purchase. Otherwise, PCs are a fraction the cost and provide all the flexibility and expandability at low costs. Never purchase a computer for its looks. Always base your decision on its capabilities and expandability. Likewise, never get involved with uncommon drives (Zip, Jazz, Superdisk, etc.) unless you have other computers with the same drives. Backup drives are virtually pointless now considering how inexpensive CD ROM RWs are (not to mention the disks have a capacity of 720 MB, are also very inexpensive, and if written properly can be read by any computer with a CD ROM which means all Pentium class or better computers).

### Advantages/Disadvantages of Manufactured

| Advantages | Disadvantages |
|---|---|
| 1. All components and software engineered together<br>2. Usually good components (reduces warranty repair costs)<br>3. Restore disk returns computer to factory settings<br>4. Warranty (one year) covers defects in components and workmanship<br>5. Technical support (limited)<br>6. Retail Technical Support<br>7. Major Software titles may be provided | 1. Limitations of expandability<br>2. Proprietary components<br>3. Proprietary driver difficulties<br>4. Most restore disks format the hard drive<br>5. Technicians must do all expansions to not void warranty |

Note: many servers do not require major equipment and merely act as share devices or firewalls (for modem sharing with a proxy server, printer or database sharing). Often a lesser manufactured machine is ideal for this use, so long as it has the capacity to hold the necessary components (e.g. Ethernet, specialized modem, the data and the system). It is also wise in an environment with many computers to retain cohesion among the computers (all made by the same manufacturer). It is particularly important in networks to be consistent with all the components.

*Advantages/Disadvantages of Custom Built*

| Advantages | Disadvantages |
|---|---|
| 1. You decide what goes in the box<br>2. Great for building high-end servers<br>3. Great for building a throw-away system (e.g. dumb terminal) cheaply | 1. Lack of support<br>2. Lack of warranty<br>3. Driver and IRQ difficulties<br>4. No factory software<br>5. Costs more to build (never use cheap parts as they will break) |

On the note of cheap parts: this is particularly a problem with motherboards, CPU fans and power supplies (AMD requires a better fan and power supply). Never go cheap on any of these three things. They will all result in unexplainable and not reproducible errors, and even total system failure.

## Expandability
The case the components are in and the motherboard will determine the expandability of your machine. Beware of half bays (where drives are docked) and multi-purpose cards. Many newer machines now provide the speaker, modem and microphone components on the motherboard. These are easy to disable independently. Multi-purpose cards often require complete disabling, which causes the card to be virtually useless. This would not be such a problem except that most of these cards must be left in the machine for the motherboard to continue functioning even after they are disabled. Most component expansions you probably want to keep internal. At present, DVD is perhaps better to leave external so you can plug the drive into your television or any computer.

## Peripherals
Be cautious about cheap peripherals. As a general rule, mid-priced monitors, printers and scanners often have great quality and reliability. Never aim low because you will be dissatisfied. The price difference is minute, so spend the extra money. The most expensive is not always best either. Nor are the best numbers. Numbers are quite misleading. When purchasing a monitor, compare its visible quality to others. Do not concern yourself with refresh rates (only Sony seems kind enough to state theirs) or dot-pitch (often large dot-pitch looks much better). Of printers, inkjets are great, but be sure they are dual cartridge with Photo Ret (do not focus on dpi), that the print heads are built into the cartridge, and compare cartridge costs. Also examine how tolerant the printer is of a variety of paper types and weights. If you plan to print greeting cards and envelopes you may want a more expensive machine with a better carriage.

### Printers
Printers come in a variety of forms with a variety of features. The table below outlines printer types and printer features to look for when making a purchase decision. Always be sure to check the printer specifications and to purchase the correct cable for the printer. Most printers do not come with a cable to connect to the computer. If the printer does come with a cable the box will be clearly marked.

| Bubble Jet | Bubble jets are small, top-feeding printers, the most common of which are manufactured by Cannon. These are typically fast with good quality, and convenient when paired with a laptop because you can fit both the laptop and a small bubble jet in a brief case with your paper. |
|---|---|
| Bursting | For printers that feed a continuous perforated sheet, pages must be separated at the perforations and edges with holes used to feed the paper must be torn off (burst) at their perforations. |
| Character Printers | Character printers are like most typewriters, physically striking a ribbon to imprint on the page. Both character and dot matrix printers are impact printers. |
| Dot Matrix | An impact printer that uses pins to form the shapes, which are then physically impacted against the ribbon onto the page. |
| dpi | A generalized term used with scanners, printers and monitors to describe the |

| | resolution in number of dots per inch.  As with a monitor, dpi refers to the number of dots used to present the output.  With the exception of laser and character printers, all printers rely on applying tiny dots on the page to draw what is being printed.  With the exception of Photo RET, the higher the dpi the better.  Be aware also that other factors affect print quality. |
|---|---|
| IEEE Cable | Also called twisted pair, but not to be confused with computer connectivity whose cables have both parallel and serial plugs on both ends.  This cable plugs in through the parallel port on your system unit then to your printer.  It is used for high speed printers like Laser printers.  On the surface it is thicker than normal parallel cable.  The reason is that each wire in the cable is wrapped in aluminum foil on top of the usual insulation.  The foil prevents cross talk, which is when wires in close proximity to each other share information they shouldn't, causing information loss and garbled communications. |
| Ink Cartridges | Ink cartridges come in a wide variety to include solids, powders, liquids, solids with liquid reservoirs, wax-based, water-based, etc.  Some come with built-in print heads, while others attach directly to a permanent print head and yet others attach to a print head changed with alternating cartridges.  If at all possible, show preference for cartridges with built-in print heads.  This typically prevents most print head problems.  When these cartridges are installed, they often require aligning, which is an utility provided with your printer's software. |
| Ink Jet | Ink Jets, through one means or another, squirt ink onto the page.  Some ink jets are splotchy, no matter how eloquent their claims about their dots.  If necessary you might take a magnifying glass with you to examine print qualities closely.  Hewlett Packard manufactures the most consistent and highest quality ink jets.  Many graphics artists also use Epson ink jets for their wide carriage prints because they are cost efficient for that kind of work.  A major difference between the manufacturers is how they feed paper.  If you plan to do a lot of heavy bond paper, wide carriage paper, or envelopes you are better off with a top feeding Epson or a high-end (800 series or above) Hewlett Packard.  The lesser Hewlett Packard's can do the job but have weaker carriages making them prone to breakage with heavy use. |
| Laser or Thermal Printers | For high-speed letter quality printing, laser printers are ideal.  While they are more costly up-front than an ink jet, and their cartridges seem to cost more, the toner cartridges last longer and you can easily use copy paper.  Laser printers are good for heavy bond papers and envelopes.  Color laser printers are rare and extremely expensive, as are laser printers with multiple trays (typically used for different paper sizes.  As a rule, laser printers are limited for printing on large paper sizes (above 8.5 X 14).  Both Hewlett Packard and Brother currently provide excellent laser printers. |
| Line Printers | Line printers are typically dot matrix, feeding through a continuous sheet of paper which requires bursting.  These are popular in industry, especially for billing and receipts because the are inexpensive to operate and maintain, and are fairly fast.  These printers do not, however, produce letter quality printing so lack application elsewhere.  Epson is notable for its line printers. |
| Multi-Function Printers | A number of ink jet printers can also scan documents, fax and make copies.  Look closely at the design of the machine to make sure it fits your needs.  Look to see if the scanner is flat, especially if you might scan items that are not normal paper sizes or may rough from age or storage.  The sheet-feeding scanners are nice (and more expensive), but it is easy to forget you are using a printer for making copies and run your cartridge bill up.  If these are not concerns, you may go cheaper with a top-feeding scanner.  Some printer-fax machines also have a keypad for manually dialing.  This is nice because then you do not need to turn on the computer to send and receive faxes. |
| Paper | We think we know about paper until we interface with the printing industry.  The most |

| | forgiving printers are Hewlett Packards, which will put out amazing quality on the worst paper (e.g. copy paper). For high-quality print jobs with any printer be mindful of your paper choices. If you are printing on a glossy surface with an ink jet it is also wise to adjust the printer properties before conducting the print, and identify the type of paper you are using. Some print jobs may require extra time for drying to prevent them from smearing as the page continues to be fed through the printer. |
|---|---|
| Paper Trays | As we noted earlier, ink jets either feed through the back on top or through the front on the bottom. In either case the finished product appears face up in the tray in front. Be sure to examine how wide the tray is, how adjustable it is, and whether it is removable. The more adjustable and wider the better, especially if you do print jobs larger than 8.5 X 11. Most Hewlett Packards provide 8.5" wide, adjustable for envelopes and for long banners. To get a wider carriage you can either divide the print job across several pages (HP provides software for this), get a more expensive HP, or save money and buy an Epson. |
| Photo-RET | A color printer with Photo-RET should always be preferred over a printer that brags only dpi. Printers without Photo-RET place dots next to each to give the illusion of colors. Photo-RET layers transparent colors on top of each other sixteen deep to get true color per dot. |
| Printer Cable | Printer cables are almost never provided with the printer. Most printers use either Parallel or USB cables. Some take both, and some only take IEEE. Be sure when purchasing a printer to check the box to see what kind of cable to purchase, and also on the off-chance that a cable is provided (which only seems to occur with very expensive printers. |
| Resolution | Resolution has many factors. For color graphics the greatest concern is the quality of the color per dot (e.g. Photo-RET), while non-color graphics (line art) are dependent on dpi. Publishers want "letter quality" which is dark and looks solid (as opposed to the grainy look of a dot matrix) and is easily achieved by setting ink jet or laser printer qualities to high (as opposed to economy, draft, or medium). |

## Scanners

Scanners come in a wider variety of forms than might be expected. Prices of flat bed scanners have plummeted making them as accessible as keyboards, though certainly more space consuming. The table below outlines the types of scanners available and scanner features to look for.

| dpi | For flat bed scanners, 1200 dpi is ideal. The file size is manageable and the quality is ideal. In reality, most scan jobs will not be able to use more than 1200 dpi because the image being scanned doesn't have a better resolution. If you scan at a resolution higher than the original, then the scanner programming is adding dots that were not there. If you are scanning slides or film, then 9600 dpi is more appropriate for that particular job. |
|---|---|
| Film | This is a rare but useful item. Do not be misled, however, as the film must first be processed. These scanners are small and specialized (not to mention expensive), capable of taking a processed roll of 35 mm film and scanning in the pictures. |
| Flat Bed Scanners | Most scanners are flat bed, capable of scanning text, graphics and pictures. Flat bed scanners are the easiest to work with because they allow the user to manage what is being scanned. A limited number of flat bed scanners are available with sheet-feeders. Many now come with buttons to initiate a scan job and send that job to a particular function of your computer, like to e-mail. |
| OCR | Object Character Recognition is now popular software provided with most scanners. OCR distinguishes between characters and graphics on a scanned image and will send that information to another program (like Word) for editing. This is extremely convenient, keeps file sizes much smaller and gives the user control over the scanned images. The technology has improved, but it is still difficult to get accurate readings |

| | on copies of copies. |
|---|---|
| Resolution | See dpi this section. |
| Single Pass | Some scanners still make three passes, one for each primary color. If at all possible avoid this attribute and get a single pass scanner. Not only does the quality seem better, you save an enormous amount of scanning time. |
| Slides (35mm) | Some flat bed scanners are or can be adapted to take 35 mm slides. The slide scanner produced by HP also scans negatives and small pictures. Again, this is a specialized and expensive commodity. |

### Monitors

Although monitors are fairly simple, there are still many things to watch out for when making your purchase decision. Monitor size is not always indicative of display size. It appears the present market has two types of good monitors: extremely expensive like the Mitsubishi or almost cheap like the Acer. The Mitsubishi has stunning (write letters to everyone you know) quality while the Acer (notably the 17"( has excellent quality at a fraction the price.

| Active Matrix | For flat screens, the active matrix is unbeatable because it refreshes only the parts of the screen that have changed. This makes tracking motion (like movement of the mouse) easy. These are also better in a wider range of lighting situations than other flat screens. |
|---|---|
| CRT | Cathode Ray Tube: the standard monitor we are all used to seeing attached to a PC. These consist of a tube just like a television, but do not have the same resolution and refresh rates as a television. You can use a television as a monitor, but you will be disappointed and even more so about the cost of the adapter. CRTs may also be plugged into laptops as an auxiliary display device. |
| Flat Color | On laptops these are adequate, though they are a little limited in bright light situations and are harder to see at angles. For regular PCs these are extremely costly and disappointing if you expect high resolution. If all you need is to save desk space and can afford to pay four times as much then a flat screen may work for you and your PC. |
| LCD | The old liquid crystal displays worked well in medium lighting and a text-driven environment with little power consumption. Today they are limited to palm-tops and calculators. |
| Refresh | The speed at which the information on the screen is replaced. For all but active matrix this means the entire screen. The only manufacturer I have seen who openly reveals their refresh rates is Sony. The refresh rate is not everything though. |
| Restore | This is typically not a monitor term but deserves particular attention here. When you change the resolutions settings of windows you will see the picture flash and show the new resolution. Most monitors will make a popping sound, as if a relay is switching physically within the monitor. Very few do not make the popping sound. Having observed this on a number of occasions, it appears a wise test of any monitor to change its resolution a few times and see how it reacts. The ones that make the popping sound are prone to failure. Some will even fail after just a few resolution changes. It appears these monitors use old-fashioned relays, while the survivors (those that do not pop) use an integrated circuit, which is more durable and less drastic. |
| Resolution | Resolution is measured in the distance between the dots on your screen, called dot-pitch. As with so many of the factors regarding monitors, the numbers can be misleading. |

## Software

If you have all your own software in full version, then software is not an issue. Otherwise it is important to see what software titles are available on the computer you purchase. Even if the software is not major, it

may be up-gradable into something that is.  For example, basic Works is expandable to Works 99 with
Word 97.  You can then use an Office upgrade rather than a full-version and save hundreds of dollars.
Other than the productivity software, encyclopedias, games, etc. are fairly cheap, so do not place too much
emphasis on them in making your purchase decision.  If you plan to play fancy 3-D games, expect to spend
money putting a 3-D Accelerator Card in your computer.  Nothing less will do.

# Worksheet 2—Hardware & Software

## Common Acronyms & Their Functions

| | | | | |
|---|---|---|---|---|
| a. | BIOS | 1. Operating System | 5. | A chip on the motherboard that identifies primary components |
| b. | CMOS | 2. Basic Input/ Output System | 6. | Changeable on startup: configures hardware and boot sequence |
| c. | FAT | 3. Graphical User Interface | 7. | Defines the number of bits per byte |
| d. | GUI | | 8. | Lays out the storage units on disks |
| e. | OS | 4. File Allocation Table | 9. | Manages system components and common program functions |
| | | | 10. | Provides file management functions |
| | | | 11. | Provides interface between hardware and applications |
| | | | 12. | User-friendly interface not requiring a keyboard |

## Memory

| | | |
|---|---|---|
| a. | Drive | 13. Temporary memory on chips |
| b. | RAM | 14. Temporary memory on a disk |
| c. | ROM | 15. Permanent memory on chips |
| d. | Shared | 16. Memory dedicated to a function |
| e. | Virtual | 17. Device for reading & writing disks |

## System Unit

| | | |
|---|---|---|
| a. | BUS | 18. Add-ons like modems |
| b. | CPU | 19. Connects chips to boards |
| c. | Expansion | 20. Connects two boards |
| d. | Motherboard | 21. Everything connects here |
| e. | Socket | 22. The actual "computer" |

## Connections I

| | | |
|---|---|---|
| a. | AGP | 23. For hard drive controller |
| b. | DIMM | 24. For memory |
| c. | IDE | 25. For video cards |
| d. | IEEE | 26. Joysticks and music keyboards |
| e. | MIDI | 27. Twisted pair, high-speed parallel |

## Connections II

| | | |
|---|---|---|
| a. | ISA | 28. Printers and scanners |
| b. | LPT | 29. Large pin expansion card slot |
| c. | NIC | 30. Memory board |
| d. | PCI | 31. Networking board |
| e. | SIMM | 32. Small pin expansion card slot |

## Plugs

| | |
|---|---|
| 33. (S)VGA | 38. For keyboards and mice |
| 34. Parallel | 39. For mice and joysticks |
| 35. PS/2 | 40. For the monitor |
| 36. Serial | 41. High speed devices |
| 37. USB | 42. Most printers: 8 bits at a time |

## Connects to...

| | | |
|---|---|---|
| a. | 10 base T | 43. Digital dedicated phone line |
| b. | Coax | 44. External drives |
| c. | COM | 45. Most networks |
| d. | ISDN | 46. Most peripherals |
| e. | SCSI | 47. Some Internet and LAN |

## Confusing Terms

| | | |
|---|---|---|
| a. | External | 48. Everything |
| b. | Internal | 49. Holds motherboard & drives |
| c. | Peripheral | 50. Outside the CPU |
| d. | System | 51. Outside the system unit |
| e. | System Unit | 52. Part of the CPU |

## CPU

| | | |
|---|---|---|
| a. | ALU | 53. Multimedia processor |
| b. | Level 1 | 54. Units for math and logic |
| c. | Level 2 | 55. Integrated circuit memory |
| d. | P III | 56. Printed circuit memory |
| e. | Pentium | 57. Class with 3-D Graphics unit |

## Speed

| | | |
|---|---|---|
| a. | # x | 58. CD & DVD ROM speeds |
| b. | bps | 59. Integrated Circuit (IC chip) speeds |
| c. | CPM | 60. Modem speed |
| d. | MHz | 61. Monitor: gap between dots |
| e. | Pitch | 62. Printer character speed |

## Disks

| | | |
|---|---|---|
| a. | DVD | 63. High-capacity optical |
| b. | Floppy | 64. High-capacity removable |
| c. | Hard/fixed | 65. Low-capacity removable |
| d. | RW | 66. Means CD is rewritable |
| e. | ZIP | 67. Non-removable |

## Printers

| | | |
|---|---|---|
| a. | Head | 68. Controls ink application |
| b. | Jet | 69. Impacts against a ribbon |
| c. | Laser | 70. Layers for true color per dot |
| d. | Line | 71. Shoots ink dots |
| e. | Photo-RET | 72. Uses heat to imprint |

## Peripheral Features

| | | |
|---|---|---|
| a. | Active Matrix | 73. Scanners & printers |
| b. | CRT | 74. Recognizes characters |
| c. | dpi | 75. Most common monitor |
| d. | LCD | 76. Common flat screen |
| e. | OCR | 77. High-quality flat screen |

## Other Office 2000 Applications

| | | |
|---|---|---|
| a. | Customer Manager | 78. Basic graphics editing |
| | | 79. Contact database like ACT! |
| b. | FrontPage | 80. Create Web pages |
| c. | PhotoDraw | 81. Special projects like business cards |
| d. | Publisher | |

## A+ Questions NOT Answered In Chapter

82. Almost all computer failure is attributable to:
    a. Hardware
    b. Software
    c. Drivers
    d. Users
    e. Viruses

83. Parity memory validates the integrity of data in RAM by
    a. Checking the header of each packet
    b. Checking each eighth bit of data
    c. Checking the RAM table in BIOS
    d. Adding the number of bits to see if they are odd or even

84. Frequent general protection faults (parity errors) may be caused by
    a. Poor quality memory chips
    b. Incorrectly connected hard drive cable
    c. Insufficient RAM
    d. All the above

85. POST stands for
    a. Power-on Startup Test
    b. Power-on Self Test
    c. Pre-Operating System Test
    d. Protected Online Startup Test

86. A continuous set of beeps indicates
    a. Keyboard error
    b. Stuck key
    c. Terminal error
    d. BIOS could not load

87. The code stored on Electronically Erasable-Programmable ROM (EEPROM) is (a)
    a. Software
    b. System
    c. Firmware
    d. Static

88. The BIOS is on the CMOS, which stands for _____ Metal Oxide Semiconductor
    a. Ceramic
    b. Complementary
    c. Continuous
    d. Capacitive

89. Removing then replacing the battery or resetting the nearby jumpers for the CMOS
    a. Erases Startup passwords
    b. Resets the BIOS to factory settings
    c. Requires re-updating BIOS settings
    d. Resets the system clock
    e. All of the above
    f. None of the above

90. A single beep during the boot sequence indicates
    a. POST is complete
    b. POST has begun
    c. POST found an error
    d. POST found no error

91. To interpret a distinct series of beeps
    a. Memorize the universal codes
    b. Look up the universal codes in any owner's manual
    c. Look up the codes in the manual for the BIOS
    d. Look up the codes in the computer or motherboard's owner's manual

92. The BIOS may be updated or written to by a virus which is called
    a. Shadowing
    b. Flashing
    c. Burning
    d. Charging
    e. Mirroring

| POST Errors | | | | Questions 100-105 Order of Hardware Failure Elimination | |
|---|---|---|---|---|---|
| 93. | Color monitor | a. | 1xx | a. | What was changed since the last time you know it worked properly? |
| 94. | Floppy disk controller | b. | 2xx | | |
| 95. | Hard disk controller | c. | 3xx | b. | What device fails under what conditions? |
| 96. | Keyboard | d. | 5xx | c. | Does the Operating System load without error? |
| 97. | Main memory | e. | 6xx | d. | Does the device conflict with another device? |
| 98. | Mouse | f. | 14xx | e. | Does POST complete without error? |
| 99. | Printer | g. | 17xx | f. | Does it power up? |
| 100. | System/Mother board | h. | 18xx | | |

| ESD (Electrostatic Discharge) | | | | DMA (Direct Memory Access) Channels | | | |
|---|---|---|---|---|---|---|---|
| 106. | Can be felt | a. | 3.3 V | 111. | Sound Card | a. | 0 |
| 107. | Can be seen | b. | +12 V | 112. | Floppy Disk Controller | b. | 1 |
| 108. | CPU voltage | c. | 30 V | 113. | 16 bit Sound Card I | c. | 1 & 3 |
| 109. | Destroys circuits | d. | 3,000 V | 114. | 16 bit Sound Card II | d. | 2 |
| 110. | Disk Drive voltage | e. | 20,000 V | 115. | Available | e. | 3 |

| Miscellaneous Errors | | | | Error Solutions | | | |
|---|---|---|---|---|---|---|---|
| 116. | Bad memory | a. | 0D | 121. | Background programs | a. | ScanDisk |
| 117. | Boot Virus or MBR error | b. | 0E | 122. | MBR errors | b. | Defrag |
| 118. | Disable background programs | c. | OS does not boot | 123. | Unable to open files | c. | fdisk /mbr |
| 119. | Needs cold boot | d. | Ultra Slow Dialogs | 124. | Ultra slow file access | d. | System Information |
| 120. | Video Error | e. | Ultra Slow Programs | | | | |

125. Lets a device bypass the CPU to get information
    a. IRQ
    b. DMA
    c. DVM
    d. I/O Address
126. You can connect __ drives to a ___ controller and ___ to a ___
    a. 2, IDE: 2.EIDE
    b. 2, IDE: 4. EIDE
    c. 4, IDE: 2, EIDE
    d. 4, IDE: 4, EIDE
127. Leave this plugged in so it is grounded when you are working on it
    a. AT Motherboards
    b. Baby AT Motherboards
    c. ATX Motherboards
    d. Monitors
    e. Both A & B
    f. Both C & D
128. Attach your ESD strap to the chassis when a grounding mat is not available to attach to on all but
    a. Motherboards
    b. Monitors
    c. Disk Drives
    d. Memory & Expansion boards
129. What electronic components store electricity and assures consistent energy supply?
    a. Capacitors
    b. Coils
    c. Resistors
    d. Varistors

130. This is a serviceable part
    a. CPU
    b. CPU Fan
    c. Power Supply
    d. System Fan
131. A grinding noise comes from the computer, which of the following could it not be?
    a. CPU Fan
    b. System Fan
    c. Disk Drive
    d. Power Supply
132. What is the operating temperature of a Pentium processor
    a. 80° F
    b. 105° F
    c. 118° F
    d. 185° F
    e. 200° F
133. Which of the following is not for cooling the CPU
    a. Mercury based thermal grease
    b. Heat Sink
    c. CPU Fan
    d. System Fan
    e. All are used
134. Energy/Green Star sleep mode reduces power consumption by
    a. 60%
    b. 80%
    c. 90%
    d. 99%

# Unit 3—System Architectures

## Objectives:
Students will understand:

| | | | |
|---|---|---|---|
| 1. | Tier Systems Architecture Model (MCSD) | 4. | Operating System Functions (MCSE & A+) |
| 2. | Networking (A+, MCSD & old MCSE) | 5. | Client/Server Architecture (MCSD) |
| 3. | Distributing Solutions (MCSD) | 6. | Use Case Solutions (MCSD) |

## Tier Systems Architecture Model (MCSD)

The Tier Model is used to describe the functional architecture of an information system. It is the classic question of: "Who does what?" The confusion about the Tier model is differentiating between which tier describes an architecture and which tier describes a component of that architecture. Most references only identify single, two and n-tiered architectures. Here I will identify four and let you fill in the blank for n-tiered system architectures.

| Architecture | Tiers | Description & Examples |
|---|---|---|
| Single Tiered | 1. Desktop computer | Applications open entire files directly (whether locally or from a network computer) without any data management conducted by a server. This is not a scalable system as the entire application, its interface and data file are transferred (over the network if one is involved). Examples would include "dumb" terminals attached to a mainframe, or a database query run on a local machine drawing the data directly from the server or other computer to function. This requires strong user knowledge and is not scalable. |
| Two Tiered | 1. Server<br>2. Client | Client-side applications access files indirectly through a server program (even if on the same machine) that directly accesses the file and regulates the data provided to the client application. This is more scalable as the server can allow multiple applications to access the same data source simultaneously and the processor on the server does not also have to manage the client-end application or interface. Examples would include a template or other document stored on a server accessed by an application on the client (even if both are on the same computer). |
| Three Tiered | 1. Data Services<br>2. Business Services<br>3. Presentation (Client) Services | Handling of data, applications and presentation are handled separately. This is extremely scalable. For example, a system where a SQL server storing the data and regulating through COM objects what is being transmitted, sends information to another server that reformats the information to be transmitted through another medium, which is then presented on the client machine. This example shows a data server level, where the raw data is directly accessed and manipulated; the raw data requested is transferred to another application like a COM object creating active server pages, which formats the information to be recognized by the user's interface application (browser) |
| Four Tiered | 1. Data Services<br>2. Business Services<br>3. Presentation Services (e.g. Web Server)<br>4. Presentation (Client) Services | Like the three-tiered architecture, this divides functions across multiple devices. Consider a high-end system where the client inputs data (interface) and another application performs manipulation on the data (3) to present it to a business server, which then applies necessary manipulations to send the data to the appropriate data server. For example, a search utility allowing users access over the Internet to query multiple sources simultaneously. The user's browser presents the interface (4). |

| | | The search utility must be able to transmit the formatted input and results pages (3). The input is received by a script (2) that reformats the query appropriate to the available search engines, submits to those engines and reformats the results into an uniform manner recognizable by the Business server. Finally, each search engine provides its own querying application managing its data warehouse to access, filter out and return the requested information. |
|---|---|---|

Note the order in which these tiers always appear: Data Services (e.g. data warehousing), Business Services (e.g. handlers, filters, web servers, etc.), and User Services (client-side applications used to present interface for input and output). At the lowest architectural tier all are on the same machine with no server involved, with a single application managing all three. At the next tier Business Services may be divided mindfully between the server and client devices (even if they are on the same machine). At Three Tiered they become more distinctly separated. At the fourth and beyond (e.g. n-Tiered) the subsets of services begin to be divided.

## Networking (A+, MCSD & old MCSE)

### OSI (Operating System Interconnection) Model Layers

The OSI (Open Systems Interconnect) Model describes the processes and architectures of networks. While we are not due to discuss networking until Lesson 8, the model is also useful in understanding software and operating systems on individual computers. From a development management perspective this helps divide large projects into meaningful parts (modules), which can be addressed separately and mapped together (e.g. data flow diagramming). From a troubleshooting and problem solving perspective this can help isolate problems.

| Layer | Description |
|---|---|
| Application | Software providing general access to network resources, flow control and error recovery for user application processes. |
| Presentation | Handles data formatting and conversion into generic format for sharing. This translates the requests from the **Application** layer into a transmittable format, then translates information received from the **Session** layer to be used by the **Application** layer. |
| Session | Allows applications to exchange information between computers by synchronizing the software. This layer handles name recognition, security, and transmission traffic, separating and marking distinct tasks to insure each task is received in order. |
| Transport | Packets information to reduce errors, error correction, flow control, etc. Tasks marked at the **Session** layer are divided or combined as necessary into packets to limit the amount of data transferred before it is checked for errors at this level on the receiving end. The packets are formed at this layer and passed to the **Network** layer, and when received this layer unpacks the information and checks for errors before passing complete tasks to the **Session** layer. |
| Network | Addresses messages for delivery and determines the transmission route based on delivery priorities. Handles packet switching/congestion control (hardware multitasking). This layer may divide packets further to compensate for physical limitations of the hardware. This layer is not responsible for any error handling. |

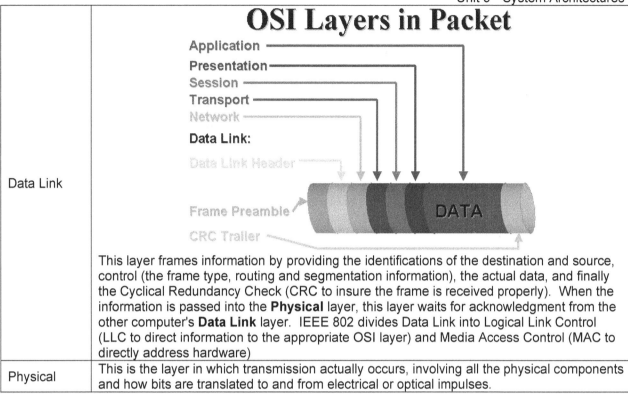

| Data Link | |
|---|---|
| | This layer frames information by providing the identifications of the destination and source, control (the frame type, routing and segmentation information), the actual data, and finally the Cyclical Redundancy Check (CRC to insure the frame is received properly). When the information is passed into the **Physical** layer, this layer waits for acknowledgment from the other computer's **Data Link** layer. IEEE 802 divides Data Link into Logical Link Control (LLC to direct information to the appropriate OSI layer) and Media Access Control (MAC to directly address hardware) |
| Physical | This is the layer in which transmission actually occurs, involving all the physical components and how bits are translated to and from electrical or optical impulses. |

Each layer acts like it is communicating directly with the same layer on the other computer. Both the OSI and Systems Architecture models provide a means to dissect and study any system and may be used to help project development.

## Hardware & Terms

| | |
|---|---|
| Bridge | Device acting at the <u>Data Link layer</u> of the OSI model, used to filter information traffic according to the packet's hardware destination address. Filters traffic between network segments. Uses MAC (hardware) addressing. |
| Brouter | Device capable of supporting both bridge and router devices and protocols. |
| Buffer | Reserved portion of memory for storing information waiting to be transmitted or received. |
| Bus Topology | System where one cable connects multiple nodes. This requires a terminating resistor to prevent the signal from bouncing back and forth and preventing other transmissions. A bus allows several independent lines to carry information simultaneously one bit at a time. |
| Crosstalk | Electomagnetic interference between adjacent communications cables resulting in mixed messages on the involved lines. |
| Duplex | Transmitting and receiving simultaneously. |
| Ethernet | A bus network topology technology. |
| Firmware | Device control software stored on the device in ROM. |
| Front/Back End | Refers to where an application is being run. Front end refers to the client computer where back end refers to the server. Back end applications tend to run faster for locating and directing data, while front end applications should be focused on the interface and output of the data. Violating either of these may lead to bottlenecking the network. |
| Gateway | Device used to connect networks who use different protocols. |
| Handshake | Information exchanged between sending and receiving devices to ensure the communication is open. Most typically used with modems. |
| Hub | A device where nodes are connected directly for a "Star" topology. An active hub |

| | |
|---|---|
| | regenerates the signals and must be powered separately. Passive hubs are less common, and acts only as a central connecting point. |
| Node | A device connected to the network that is also capable of communicating with other network devices (e.g. a server, client, or repeater). |
| Router | Device operating at the <u>Network layer</u> of the OSI model, allowing connection of different physical media, translating between different network architectures, such as token ring and Ethernet. |
| Rule, 5-4-3 | Coaxial ethernets can have a maximum of 5 cable segments, 4 repeaters, and 3 populated segments. |
| Spanning Tree Algorithm | Method of determining the shortest route between two network computers, eliminating redundant routes which are reactivated if the primary route becomes unavailable. |
| Synchronous Transmission | Method of transmitting information using time as a factor rather than start and stop bits. It is faster, more efficient and more expensive than asynchronous transmission (which sends one character at a time over variable time frames and with fixed frame sizes and start and stop bits). |

## *TCP/IP in Extreme Brief*

### Overview

Protocols: method of communicating
- Why Protocols?
- Network Setup (Windows)
- Protocol Properties

1

### Why Protocols?

- Hardware recognition
  - Routers, Hubs, Network Interface Cards
- Uniform Interface
  - Machine Language Compatibility
- Identify Communication Types
  - HTTP, E-mail, File & Program Sharing
- Information Packeting
  - Multitasking servers, Error Correction
- Security
  - Fire Walls, user identity and access level

2

### Network Setup
#### (Windows 95 and above)

- Install NICs and connect computers
- Install Network Neighborhood
- Add Adapter to Network Neighborhood
- Add Protocol to Network Neighborhood
- Modify Protocol Properties

3

### Install Network Neighborhood

Although not normally necessary:
- Start + Settings + Control Panel
- Double Click Add/Remove Programs
- Click the Windows Setup tab
- Select Communications Option
- Click OK

4

## Setting up a Client Computer

- Access Network Properties
- Add Protocols
- Identify Computer and Workgroup
- Define Access Levels for other computers
- Adjust Protocol Properties

5

## Network Properties

- Right Click

Network Neighborhood

- Select Properties
- Click Add...

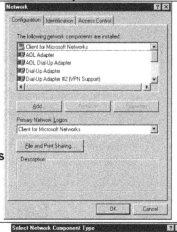

6

## Identification

- Computer name
- Workgroup name
- Computer description

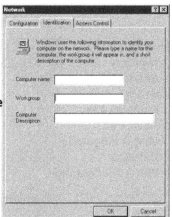

7

## Adding Protocols

- Select Protocol
- Click Add...
- Select Microsoft
- Scroll down on right
- Select TCP/IP
- Click OK

8

## ARPANet & TCP/IP

- Advanced Research Project Agency
- Department of Defense
- Transmission Control Protocol (TCP) 1973
- TCP/IP standard Internet Protocol since 1983

9

## Network Configuration

Setup network elements:
- Clients
- Adapters
- Services
- Protocols

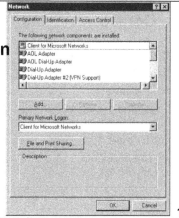

10

## Adapter

- Identifies the hardware (NIC)
- Identifies the connection type
  - Dial-up, direct connection
- Bindings (root interface protocols)
  - IPX/SPX, NetBEUI
- Network usage logs and IPX compression

11

## Clients

- Identifies individual using computer
- Identifies logon method
  - Windows startup or when network is accessed
- Identifies location of logon validation
  - Local computer or network domain

12

## Services

- **Share files and printers**
- **Automatic system backup**
- **Remote registry**
- **Network monitor**

13

## Protocol Properties

- Select Protocol
- Click Properties
- Modify:
  - Gateway
  - Subnet Mask
  - IP Address
  - Bindings Tab
  - Advanced
  - DNS Configuration
  - NetBIOS
  - WINS Configuration

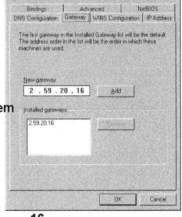

14

## Access Control

**Itemized resource sharing:**

- Share-level
  - general access to specified resources
- User-level
  - limit access to individuals

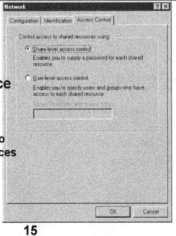

15

## Gateway

Perspectives:
- Hardware
- Operating System

16

| Gateway (Hardware) | Gateway (Operating System Perspective) |
|---|---|
| Hardware perspective:<br>• The hub or router<br>• Connects clients to server – or –<br>• Connects peer-to-peer clients<br>• Allows unlike computers to communicate<br><br><br>17 | • Identifies the interface server<br> – Uses four-part number like 2.59.20.16<br> – Each part's number range: 0-255<br> – Each part occupies one byte (8 bits)<br>• Provides:<br> – Default routing of data<br> – Protocol management with interface<br>• Multiple Gateways are prioritized   18 |
| **Gateway Similarities** | **Gateway Source** |
| • Internal digital phone lines<br> – Consist of a block of (multiple) numbers<br> – One number "revolves"<br> – Keeps other lines open<br> – Acts as telephone "gateway"<br> – i.e. 1-480-555-1212<br><br><br>19 | • All servers attached to the Internet are assigned an IP (Internet Protocol) by InterNIC associated with the DNS<br>• Local Gateway is first four numbers of the DNS IP<br>• Each number occupies one byte<br>• Example: 2.59.20.16<br>• Binary Equivelant:<br>00000010.00111011.00010100.00010000  20 |

# DNS

**Domain Name System Components:**
• **Host computer (Gateway)**—www.
• **Domain name (IP port on host)**—microsoft
• **Suffix (to access DNS registry)**—.com
(note: .com indicates InterNIC registry)
**Configuration Settings:**
• **Order of locations used to convert Domain Names to IP Addresses**

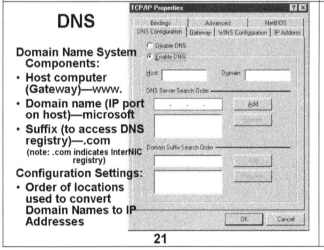

21

# Subnet Mask

• **Similarities:**
 – Image masking to hide colors
 – Telephone extensions
• **Hides local network address (IP)**
• **Contains local computer interactions**
• **Consists of four numbers (octets)**
 – I.e. 255.255.252.0

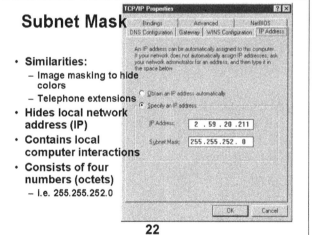

22

# Subnet Examples

- **Telephone area code switches**
  - Gateway = 1-480-555
  - Subnet = 1-480
  - Subnet Mask hides subnet for local calls
- **Internal Digital Telephone System**
  - Uses extensions as subset of phone number: 1-480-555-1212-123
  - Gateway: 1-480-555-1212
  - Internal calls mask Gateway
  - External calls use 9 to override Gateway

23

# Masking Methods

- **Gateway example: 2.59.20.16**
  00000010.00111011.00010100.00010000
- **Subnet Mask: 255.255.252.0**
  11111111.11111111.11111100.00000000
- **Local numbers are last** ten digits
- **To calculate binary numbers use** Calculator **from Accessories submenu**

24

# IP Address

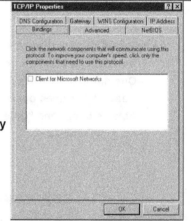

- **Similar to a telephone extension**
- ID number **attached to the** unmasked **part of the** Gateway
  - I.e. 2.59.20.234
  - Number range: 0-255
- **ID number is a Port on a** Gateway
- **Cannot be replicated in network**

25

# Bindings

- **Components using TCP/IP**
- **Improve performance by minimizing number of components selected**

26

# Advanced

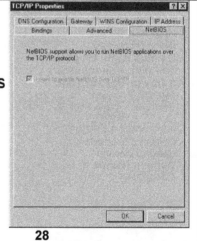

- **Allows user to set current protocol as default for selected items**
- **Determines which protocol is default**
- **NetBEUI is default on installation**

27

# NetBIOS

- **Used with WINS and DNS for naming IP addresses on the network.**

28

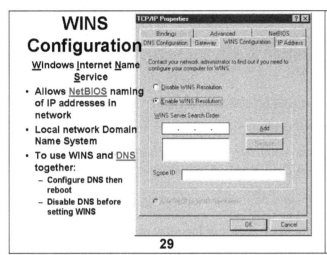

## WINS Configuration

Windows Internet Name Service

- Allows NetBIOS naming of IP addresses in network
- Local network Domain Name System
- To use WINS and DNS together:
  - Configure DNS then reboot
  - Disable DNS before setting WINS

29

## Summary

**To fill communications needs:**

- **TCP provides:**
  - Information Packeting
  - Uniform Interface
- **Gateways provide:**
  - Hardware recognition
  - Variety in communication types
- **Subnet Masks maintain internal communications**
- **IP Addresses provide Internal Security:**
  - Computer Identity and access level

30

In Windows 2000, with Active Directory's NAT (Network Address Translation) system, local (unregistered) IP addresses can be arranged as follows: 10.{0-255}.{0-255}.{1-255} or 172.16.{0-255}.{1-255} or 192.168. {0-255}.{1-255}. Note NAT runs as either a DHCP or DNS server (for name resolution) or both, but cannot be used for Internet addressing. A registered IP address is necessary for the NAT Windows server to have shared connection with the Internet.

## Distributing Solutions (MCSD)

### Distribution Alternatives

| Method | Description |
|--------|-------------|
| Floppy Disk | There is seldom much use for floppy disks anymore, particularly in application distribution for multiple reasons. The main reasons are: high-speed network connections (even through the Internet), application size and technical know-how. Even simple data files are often too large to distribute using floppy disks. Floppy disks should be limited to small-size distribution where network connections are unreliable or bandwidth is already overwhelmed. Users need some degree of technical know-how, or an installation program with printed instructions to insure proper use. |
| CD-ROM | A more likely distribution, where network connections are unreliable or bandwidth use is high is by CD-ROM. This can be done with even less technical know-how because an installation program can be executed using an autorun.inf. CDs can store up to 650 megabytes. Typically this really means 599 megabytes because the table of contents for the CD consumes the rest of the available disk. I would discourage the use of rewritable CDs for multiple reasons. First, you must be certain any CD-ROM drive that will use a CD-RW is a multiread (and this is uncommon). Second, CD-RWs lose space with every rewrite and can only be reused 99 times. As such it would be more advisable to use JAZZ or Zip disks (which of course requires the recipients have the drives too. |
| Web | A pull method requiring the user to access an Active Server Page (ASP) where the page can do some analysis and the user can identify their system configuration to insure the application is installed correctly. Failure to use an ASP may result in users installing the wrong application. |
| Pull | The client requests installation of an application or file stored on a server computer. Typically you would only use this method if you do not expect the clients to use the file or application. |
| Push | The server forces installation of an application or file on a client computer. Use this when you expect the clients to have the file or application. |

### Systems Management Server (SMS)

| Features | • Select which clients receive an application and when (forced)<br>• Spread the workload across the network to other files servers<br>• Schedule and push installations on<br>• Track installation progress<br>• Monitor what applications are installed on clients listed in the SMS Inventory database |
|---|---|
| Requirements | • SMS Package Command Manager installed on clients<br>• SMS installed on a primary domain controller on an NTFS partition with at least 500 megabytes of available space (1 gigabyte recommended)<br>• Windows NT or 2000 server<br>• SQL Server 6.0 or later (with login and permission to create and maintain a SQL database) to store the SMS Inventory<br>• Additional space on file servers for three copies of the software to be distributed |
| Recommended | • SMS Installer (get separately from www.microsoft.com) to package, automate and modify installation tasks (even proposed registry entries).<br>Run SMSIMAIN.exe to install the installer files then run SMSINSTL.exe to install |
| How it Deploys | • You check the SMS Inventory to verify software and operating systems on clients.<br>• You determine what they need and create a package definition specifying what is executed to begin installation, set installation options and store the package on one or more (preferably 3) distribution servers.<br>• You create a Job specifying which package to send and to which clients, the options to select and the locations of the distribution servers where the application is stored.<br>• The job is sent to the client and appears in the Package Manager, where it is executed and the status of the installation is reported back to the SMS server.<br>• When the job is executed the client computer retrieves the package from the distribution server, and upon arrival initiates the installation.<br>• Finally the status is reported back to the SMS server |

## Operating Systems (MCSE & A+)

### Function

On the architecture model the operating system always resides at the application services layer, even if that layer is integrated with other services. All operating systems have the given qualities:
- A File Allocation Table (FAT) to define how data is stored and retrieved from storage media
- Chipset (memory and CPU) management
- User Interface (textual or graphical)
- File management utilities (e.g. deleting, moving, renaming files and folders/directories, and creating folders/directories)
- Software to interface with hardware
- A software platform (kernel) in which other software can be run
- Computer communications/networking capabilities

On IBM compatible systems, Windows 95 introduced pre-emptive multitasking. With DOS the operating system had no control over the CPU, so a frozen application meant rebooting the system. Since Windows 95 the CPU has retained control so a misbehaving program can be disconnected from the CPU without a complete shutdown. Another feature of pre-emptive multitasking was the ability of the operating system to offer the same services to multiple applications even if those services did not come with the operating system. These are commonly seen in the form of DLLs (Dynamic Link Libraries), COM (not .com) and DCOM objects. In previous operating systems this meant that library functions were embedded and compiled in the program. With this system the operating system calls the function into memory when it is needed and can then release it when it is no longer in use. Besides providing portability in RAM, secondary storage space is also conserved. Each service contains a unique identification (UUID or GUID), which is stored in the system registry. When a program needs the service it makes the request for the ID through the operating system.

Other intimate and useful features of modern operating systems are also stored in the system registry. For example, association of file extensions with the application required to view and/or edit the file. The personalized layout of the Graphical User Interface is also stored in the registry, as is the hardware profile both past and present. Note: updates to the registry occur when Windows shuts down and recognize when the system reboots.

While modern operating systems provide at least some degree of networking capability, earlier systems often required more software. Since the introduction of multimedia processors (Pentium class CPUs) operating systems have provided at minimum dial-up-networking capabilities with TCP/IP, IPX/SPX, and NetBEUI protocols to enable network communications, file and hardware sharing. The more current the system, the more refined this networking capability (TCP/IP had to be installed through the Network Neighborhood in 98, while it is installed by default in ME and 2000). Modern computers are assumed to become members of a network, the least of which is the Internet.

Operating systems since Windows 95 have included "plug-and-play" hardware recognition. This has proven problematic as three conditions are required for plug-and-play to work: plug-and-play BIOS, plug-and-play operating system, and plug-and-play device. In spite of this, plug-and-play devices can still experience conflicts with other devices. Fortunately one of the wonderful features of plug-and-play includes the ability to modify the resource requirements (IRQ and I/O Addressing) of a device without having to pull the device out and change physical jumpers or dipswitches. Only PCMCIA are guaranteed to have 100% plug-and-play capabilities, so much that you can "hot-dock" them (plug them in while the system is on) and they will recognize.

The system BIOS has also advanced to automatically recognize and use more devices (e.g. the CD ROM). This does not, however, remove the need for the operating system to regulate these devices and provide separate drivers for them. Drivers give the devices greater versatility so the user can customize how applications communicate and use the devices.

### *OSI Approach to Architecture*

| | | |
|---|---|---|
| Application | Win32 | Native application for Windows 95-2000. |
| | Win16 | Native to Windows 3.x. All run in same Virtual DOS Machine (VDM) and share same memory allocation in 95 and later. As such, if one fails all fail. |
| | DOS | 8-bit applications run in separate VDMs. VDMs are awckward because applications originally in DOS were designed to directly address hardware. Windows 95 and above forbid this (see preemptive multitasking above) |
| | OS/2 | Version 1.x, 16 bit character based, real-mode applications only. These run in their own space or can be run in the VDM by using Forcedos.exe. |
| | POSIX | Portable Operating System Interface for Computer Environments (specifically UNIX) standard Version 1.x compliant applications only; run in own space. |
| | Logon | Integral element of Windows security, and as such runs in its own space. |
| Presentation | Subsystems | OS/2, Win32, POSIX, and Security. Responsible for establishing memory allocation, running their respective applications and establishing the Session. Note: Security/Integral is specific to Active Directory Services. |
| Session | Win32 | Provides user interface and screen functions for all applications. OS/2, POSIX, and Security subsystems otherwise address the Kernel. For VDM and Win32, Win32 Session spans the Presentation layer to provide Subsystem services including interfacing with the Kernel. |
| ▲User Mode▲ | | ▼Kernel Mode▼ |

| Transport | Executive Services—manages information and instruction transfers between user mode and kernel and between kernel components (see diagram below). |
| --- | --- |
| Network | Procedural managers regulating operating system functions. |
| Data Link | I/O and Window managers span from the Network. I/O manages the memory, file system and device drivers. Window manager handles graphics and the video adapter. All other Network layer managers rely on the Microkernel to manage IRQs, multi-task management and threading (running only the necessary parts of a program). The Hardware Abstraction Layer (HAL) allows the Microkernel to see all hardware platforms as the same. The diagram below associates the Microkernel to the Logical Link Control and the HAL to the Media Access Layer (MAC). |
| Physical | All hardware in the system. |

**Windows 2000 Architecture**

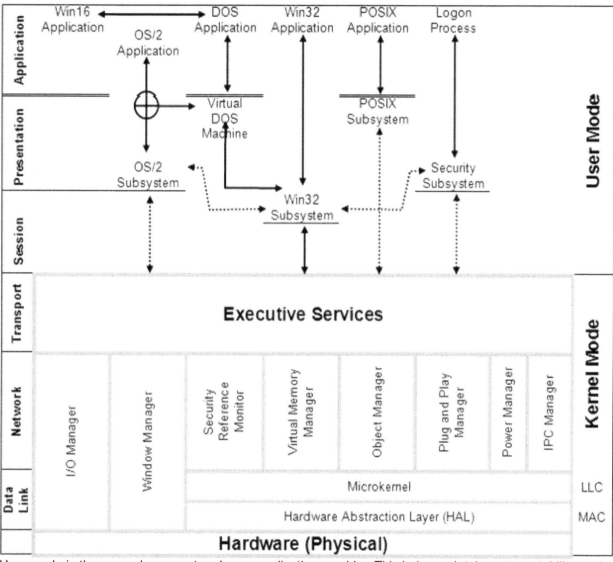

User mode is the area where most end-user applications reside. This helps maintain system stability as the kernel protects the main body of the operating system and insures the operating system retains control of the hardware. This is why application failure is not normally terminal in Windows, but when a hardware device driver fails the system becomes unstable and should be rebooted (cold is always best to insure complete reallocation of resources). The easiest source of these failures is through the I/O and Window managers because they span the Network and Data Link layers and have a lot to do for user mode applications. Kernel mode is considered "highly privileged" and you must be mindful of its weaknesses.

# Worksheet 3—System Architectures

| **Tier Cases** | a. Single-Tier | b. Two-tier | c. N-tier |
|---|---|---|---|

1. An accounting program for a large corporation that must retrieve data from branch offices and display them as charts and graphs. The application serves several hundred users worldwide.
2. A program generating monthly reports from data stored on the departmental server down the hall. The reports are complex, so the user interface for the program needs to be both complex and responsive. Only a few users will use the program.
3. A custom made front-end program accessing a database running on the same machine.
4. An enterprise application allowing access to data on a single server by branch offices worldwide.
5. A Web-based on-line "shopping cart" displaying product information, calculates price for each order entered, and stores order information in a database.

6. Problems found in single-tiered systems include (select all that apply)
   a. Complicated server-side stored procedures
   b. High network traffic loads
   c. Poor maintainability
   d. Poor scalability
7. Advantages of a two-tiered system include: (select all that apply)
   a. Database structural independence
   b. Protected access
   c. Rubricated processing theorems
   d. Stored procedures
8. On a single-tiered architecture the client application uses the server as:
   a. A basic file source
   b. A direct link to search engines
   c. A remote link to multiple data services
   d. A source for interactive graphics operations
9. Migration from single to two-tiered architectures...
   a. Can be accomplished incrementally
   b. Is prohibitively expensive
   c. Makes single-tiered applications obsolete
   d. Requires complete replacement of client-side systems

10. Two tiered architecture...(select all that apply)
    a. Client-side applications make intelligent queries and display the results
    b. Higher network loads supporting complex queries
    c. No direct access by the client to the database
    d. Server-side applications process queries and return the information
11. Single-tiered applications depend on...
    a. A detailed knowledge of the structure of the database accessed
    b. Intelligent responses to queries
    c. Responses supplied by stored procedures
    d. The server-side computing power to locate and format data
12. Three-tiered architectures: (select all that apply)
    a. Allow multiple clients to access the same data simultaneously
    b. Easily scalable using component objects
    c. Demand large increases in network resources
    d. Use object methods and sharing tasks across more than two systems

| **Services Cases** | a. Presentation Services | b. Application Services | c. Data Services |
|---|---|---|---|

For these consider a three-tier enterprise application consisting of a cluster of servers running a SQL database, a Web server with a set of business objects, and clients who access the system with their browsers on Windows operating systems.

13. SQL database
14. Windows front-end
15. Web server
16. Web browser

17. An order-processing component
18. Object on the second cluster of servers designed to retrieve the contents of a table from the SQL database

## Layers of the Open Systems Interconnect (some answers used more than once)

| | |
|---|---|
| 19. The correct order of the OSI layers is ____, ____, ____, ____, ____, ____, and ____ <br><br> 20. The layer responsible for routing where a packet goes. <br> 21. The layer responsible for creating the packet. <br> 22. The layer responsible for formatting the packet. <br> 23. The layer responsible for synchronizing the applications on the networked computers. <br> 24. Contains the sub layers of Media Access Control (MAC) and Logical Link Control (LLC). | a. Application <br> b. Data Link <br> c. Network <br> d. Physical <br> e. Presentation <br> f. Session <br> g. Transport |

| Processing in Networks | | Sending & Receiving in Networks | |
|---|---|---|---|
| a. Absolute<br>b. Call<br>c. Local Execution<br>d. Relative<br>e. Remote | 25. Localized reference not requiring name/IP resolution<br>26. Reference requiring name/IP resolution<br>27. Request for information from the server.<br>28. Using the CPU of another computer to run a program<br>29. Using the CPU to run an program received from another computer | 30. Division of the information being exchanged<br>31. Method of packaging information to be exchanged between computers<br>32. Means and rate information is exchanged<br>33. Sending information received from one computer to another<br>34. Whenever information is exchanged | a. Transmission<br>b. Relaying<br>c. Protocol<br>d. Packet<br>e. Connection |

35. The Open Systems Interconnection standard provides:
    a. Five-layer protocol standards for e-mail
    b. Seven layer protocol standards for networking framework communications
    c. A very tight definition of standards
    d. The only open standard for application development

36. When should floppy disks be used to distribute applications? (select 2)
    a. When the application must be deployed quickly
    b. When the application is small
    c. To install on multiple clients simultaneously
    d. When the network connection is unreliable

37. What product must be installed on the network before SMS?
    a. Access
    b. FoxPro
    c. SQL Server
    d. IIS

38. What would be the most reliable way to install an application on networked computers typically running at 90% bandwidth capacity?
    a. Push Install
    b. SMS
    c. Pull Install
    d. CD-ROM

39. When packages are distributed using SMS, where do the clients get the files?
    a. Distribution Server
    b. SQL Server
    c. SMS Server
    d. Package Server

40. What method is most efficient for installing large applications over a slow-networked link?
    a. CD-ROM
    b. Network
    c. Web-based
    d. SMS package

41. Where can you send packages created in SMS?
    a. Any Windows computer on the network
    b. Any SMS Server
    c. Any computer in the SMS inventory
    d. Any computer in the SMS domain

42. How do you automate a web-based installation for a variety of recipients?
    a. Provide links for each type of client
    b. Create an Active Server Page
    c. Create a form for the client to set parameters
    d. Installation must be the same for all clients

43. What types of installation must be initiated by the client?
    a. Push installation
    b. SMS Package
    c. Web-based installation
    d. SMS Installer

44. What types of clients can have software installed through SMS?
    a. Netware servers
    b. OS/2 clients
    c. NT servers
    d. DOS clients

45. How do you track those who received SMS packages?
    a. Check the registries of the clients
    b. Use the Package Locator application
    c. Check the SMS inventory database
    d. E-mail each client

46. How can you force installation on an SMS client?
    a. Include the command in the logon script
    b. Create a package with mandatory installation time
    c. Create a Must Install package
    d. Explicitly state clients must receive the application

47. How much storage do you need on an SMS server to distribute an application?
    a. The application plus 100 MB for overhead
    b. Just for the application
    c. The application plus three copies
    d. The application plus one copy for each 100 clients

48. How can you determine which clients need an upgrade?
    a. Inventory the clients through SMS
    b. Roll out the upgrade one department at a time
    c. Search client registries
    d. Scan client file systems
49. What features does SMS include?
    a. Software metering
    b. Software distribution
    c. Software inventory
    d. Remote control
50. Minimize network traffic by …(select all that apply)
    a. Centralizing all components
    b. Distributing components evenly throughout the system
    c. Ensuring the network uses high-band-pass filters
    d. Putting components at their point of use
51. Server-side business logic…
    a. Allows server administrators to monitor transactions
    b. Compensates for the lack of computing power in thin-clients
    c. Prevent unauthorized access to databases
    d. Reduce the amount of traffic on the network
52. Deployment factors to consider: (select all that apply)
    a. Application internationalization
    b. Component interoperability
    c. Locality of the reference
    d. Shipping costs
53. Rules that should be observed for components and services include: (select all that apply)
    a. Always purchase components to supply pre-built services
    b. Distribute services evenly across the full range of components
    c. Group services invoked together in the same component
    d. Keep services not invoked together in separate components
54. Client/server solution architectures include: (select all that apply)
    a. Distributed component
    b. Multi-server
    c. Multi-tiered
    d. Single-tiered
55. After testing a deployment, roll out the application to:
    a. All the clients
    b. A half-dozen clients
    c. All clients on a network segment
    d. A limited number of mixed clients

56. Distributed solutions must consider: (select all that apply)
    a. Compatibility
    b. Geographical distribution
    c. International export controls
    d. Network loads
57. Which of the following should influence your choice of technologies? (choose all that apply)
    a. Application requirements
    b. Currently installed technologies
    c. Your team's current expertise
    d. All of the above
    e. None of the above
58. In production your application will run on a cluster of high-powered multiprocessor servers. On what should you test your application?
    a. A single desktop machine
    b. A multiprocessor desktop machine
    c. Two multiprocessor machines
    d. On the production servers
59. The proper method for installing your application on the production servers is:
    a. Plan the rollout and execute the plan on the production servers
    b. Use an automated tool to install directly to the production servers
    c. Plan the rollout, practice the rollout on the test machines, then execute the plan on the production servers
    d. Plan the rollout, remove all test software (including DLLs and system component) from the test servers, practice the rollout on the test machines, then execute the plan on the production servers
60. What is the best action for your application to take if more users access it than it was designed to handle?
    a. Shut down, then start up later and see if usage has decreased
    b. Fill the database with error codes to signal the system operator for help
    c. Shut down and reboot the server to release the excess connections
    d. Refuse new connections with an easy-to-understand error message and continue processing requests from current connections

# Unit 4—Logic

## Objectives:
Students will understand:

| | |
|---|---|
| 1. Logic Basics | 3. Flowcharting |
| 2. Logic of Reality | 4. Logical Syllogism |

## Logic Basics

### Set Theory

| | | |
|---|---|---|
| Euler's Circles | System of using circles to illustrate relationships of sets. For example, all pine trees (subset) are trees (set) but not all trees are pine trees. | |
| Set | A group of objects related by definition. {a, b, c} | |
| Subset | A group of objects representing only parts of the definition of a larger group. {a, b } ⊆ {a, b, c, d }. Proper subsets: A ⊂ B iff A ⊆ B && A ≠ B | |
| Join/Union | Those values that belong to one or both related sets. {a, b, c} ∪ {b, c, d} = {a, b, c, d} | |
| Difference | The non-corresponding qualities of two sets. {a, b, c} \ {y, b, z} = {a, c, y, z} | |
| Element | A component definition item of an object. **hair ∈ mammals** | |
| Intersect | A point in space where two sets have the same value. {a, b, c} ∩ {b, c, d} = {b, c} | |
| Complement | The part of a related set not part of the relationship. A={a, b, c} & B={b, c, d} ∴ A'={a} | |

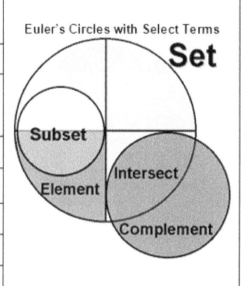

Euler's Circles with Select Terms

Set
Subset
Intersect
Element
Complement

| | | |
|---|---|---|
| Ring | A set containing two or more sets including the union and differences of the sets. The example illustrates a ring containing the three sets of mammals. Live birth is a difference between most mammals and both the platypus and all marsupials. | |
| && | Boolean "AND." All mammals have: **hair && mammary glands.** | |
| \|\| | Boolean "OR." Mammal births are: **live \|\| marsupial \|\| egg.** | |
| ! | Boolean "NOT." **Mammals !Australia=live birth.** However the illustration does fail to show that Australian mammals may also give live birth. | |

Ring of Mammals

Womb-Live Birth
Water
Land
Hair & Mammary Glands
Lay Eggs
Australia
Marsupial

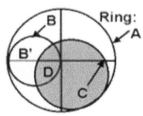

Ring: A
B
B'
D
C

Complement: B'= B- C

Intersection: D=B ∩ C

Union:
B ∪ C = B' + C' + D

Difference:
B \ C = B + C - D

## Aggregate Symbols

Symbols are used to contain, always indicating the contents should be treated as a unit.

| | |
|---|---|
| ( ) | Parentheses—Most common symbol for algebraic grouping. For example 2*3+4=10 while 2*(3+4)=14. In mapping/graphing parentheses commonly indicate open (not on minima or maxima) coordinates like (x, y). Parentheses are also commonly used in the declaration of a class in programming, like SortClass(). |
| [ ] | Brackets—typically used in mathematics to better show a coordinate as closed (on maxima or minima). |
| { } | Braces—often used to illustrate a set. In programming these often surround groups of code, like the body of an IF statement, or the code within a class. |

## More Necessary Symbols

| | | | |
|---|---|---|---|
| ≅ | Approximate equality | ≠ | Mathematical symbol for inequality |
| ≈ | Approximate equality | ∅ | Null or empty set (note: ∅ ≠ 0) |
| ∉ | Indicates an item is not an element of a set. a ∉ {b, c, d} | ± | Used to indicate a value may have either value polarity. |
| ∋ | Mathematical shorthand for "such that" (e.g. a statement of conditions applied to the results of a function). | ∓ | Used to indicate reversal of value polarity. For example a positive value going in would be negative coming out. |
| ≡ | Congruence indicates the result is the same but the original variables were different (equivalence). For example 1/4 ≡ 3/12. | ⊄ | Indicates the set on the left is not a subset of the set on the right. |
| | | ∴ | Mathematical shorthand indicating a conclusive or deductive "therefore." |
| Δ | Symbol indicating change. | $f$ | Common symbol used to indicate a function of a variable (e.g. $f(x)$). |

## Programming Symbols

| | |
|---|---|
| == | Logical argument testing for equality between two values or calculations. |
| != | Logical argument testing for inequality (≠) between two values or calculations. |
| ?: | Ternary Operator—a linear function that tests an instance then provides true and false results. The function must be contained in a line of code and nesting is not possible. e.g. [logical test]?[true result]:[false result] |
| <= | Logical argument testing two values to determine if the value on the left is less than or equal to the value on the right. |
| >= | Logical argument testing two values to determine if the value on the left is greater than or equal to the value on the right. |

## Graphing

| | |
|---|---|
| Edge | A line connecting two vertices (a vertex pair); denoted with an **E**. On a polyhedron the number of edges enclosing a single face is denoted with an **S**. |
| Face | An area outlined by edges; denoted with an **F**. Graphs illustrating the shortest route traveled among points without intersecting the same point twice do not have enclosed faces unless the traveler returns to the point of origin or a "hub" is used. |
| Graph | An illustration of a group of related vertices or "points." |
| Line | An infinite series of adjoined points defining a length or arc. |
| Point | A location in space typically defined by coordinates, e.g. (x, y), (x, y, z), or (ρ, θ). When applied to a polygon or polyhedron, points are typically given for vertices. In mathematics |

| | a point has no dimension in itself. |
|---|---|
| Polygon | The geometric, two-dimensional shape resulting from connecting vertices. |
| Polyhedron | The topological, three-dimensional shape resulting from connecting vertices. |
| Vertice | A point in space that may be connected to other points by two or more lines; denoted with a V. |

## *Validity and Reliability*

| | |
|---|---|
| Domain | The minimum and maximum X values of a function. |
| Range | The minimum and maximum Y values of a function. |
| Reliable | State of providing the correct results. Although a function may be valid (performing the correct action), the results may not always be correct. Most mathematical operations on computers follow valid algorithms for their solutions. However, computers have limited data capacities, causing larger numeric operations to fail. e.g. finding the exact value for pi ($\pi$). |
| Valid | State of performing the expected task correctly. |

## Logic of Reality

An axiom is a self-evident truth, such as: all sets belong to an universal set of sets, and the universal set of sets belongs to itself. Axioms cannot be proved nor disproved. A paradox (a.k.a. tautology) is an axiom that appears in contradiction, such as Axiom 11 below. Axioms fall into three categories: holistic (applies to everything always), particular (applies conditionally to only specific things at specific times, such as: Do unto others as <u>they</u> would have you do unto <u>them</u>), and definitive (applies to concepts and descriptive terms). Axioms rely strongly on the logic of predicates (the object of a claim) and propositions (the subject/claim asserted about the object). Statements with one predicate are monadic (Axioms 1 & 2), two or more are polyadic (note after Axiom 1). The combination of these must be carefully considered in the creation of axioms to prevent semantic skewing of meaning. Axioms are inductive, meaning they assert a generalized formula about many things based on a single thing. The following selected axioms are taken from the Unified Field Theory:

Axiom 1.    An axiom is a <u>self-evident truth</u>.  (note: the underlined is the <u>predicate</u>, the rest is the *proposition*)

Axiom 2.    All objects of mind and physical reality are <u>processes</u>.

Axiom 3.    All objects have an antithesis of what they are not.

Axiom 4.    All objects are related to each other.

Axiom 5.    All processes have the measurable (paralogical) component processes of affective, effective and effectual *Axis* (axiological).

Axiom 8.    Though the parts constitute the whole, only the whole completely represents itself (note previous verbiage: The whole is greater than its parts.)

Axiom 9.    The whole is a function of its parts. (note previous verbiage: The whole is the sum of its parts.)

Axiom 10.    Each part or group of parts may be studied as a whole in themselves.

Axiom 11.    An infinite quantity of finite values exists, while a finite quantity of infinite values exists.

Axiom 12.    Though a definable set contains infinite dimension, the set remains singular and necessarily finite.

Axiom 13.    All values are inferred through projection relative to paralog measures of axiologs.

Axiom 16.    The conservation of values within dimensions is a function of the processes relating them. (note previous law of conservation: The sum quantity of all energy (mass) remains constant while values are converted between forms of the same (e.g. energy or mass).)

Axiom 18.    All processes exist in a state of entropic change.

Axiom 19.    The antithesis of zero is one; the antithesis of one is infinity; the antithesis of infinite is zero. (Thus the Holistic is its own antithesis. A non-mathematical version would be: The antithesis of nothing is something; the antithesis of something is everything; the antithesis of everything is nothing; thus the absolute totality is its own antithesis.)

Axiom 20.    A complete Paradigm contains parallel properties that unfold and enfold.

     Axioms are not typically seen as debatable, provable, or capable of being disproved. The semantic may wish to argue with some verbiage (e.g. Axiom 4--not being related is also a relationship). Many of the axioms stated here are not easily apprehended on a concrete level, but nowhere does it say that self-evident requires any particular level of knowledge or abstract capabilities. These are self-evident from my observations, studies and experiences. These axioms, though often not easily apprehended, contain an expressed or implied "all" and "always," meaning independent of situation and time. When a statement has a particular application alone, then I classify it as a proposition (e.g. specific mathematical operations), which is an arguable and particular axiom. The reader will note these axioms clearly define a transcendent metaphysics. Notice also that occasionally I identify previous axioms which these supplant. The verbiage differences may be slight, but are quite significant.

     Advocates of infinite may wish to object to these axioms, but may have some difficulty pinpointing where to aim their objection. These axioms neither condemn nor advocate the theory of infinite. Axiom 11 is double barreled, shooting both extremities with equal prejudice. The processes advocated here are continuous (infinite) and "closed" (finite) in atomistic quanta, which are indefinitely divisible into other objects of different quanta. While point has advantages in mathematics, quantum members are finite, manageable and relative to identifiable definitions. Atomistic quanta are wholes in themselves, whose constituent processes present other quanta and are infinite in the cycles of their quantum processes.

     Axiom 19 presents a tautology through a three-step system: $f(0) = \infty$; $f(\infty) = 1$; $f(1) = 0$. The Holistic takes on the form arguments $f(f(0), f(\infty), f(1)) = (f(\infty), f(1), f(0)) = (1, 0, \infty) \equiv (0, \infty, 1) \equiv (\infty, 1, 0)$, etc. because of relativity (Axiom 13) and conservation (Axiom 16). Hence, Axiom 20 does not contradict Axiom 3. We have three values in this argument because of Axioms 5 and 13. The more pressing questions this raises is: "How do we mathematically define the function $f$?" and, "What would the value of $f(x)$ equal?" We note that the derivative $\infty_{-\infty} = \infty/\infty = 1$, and $1_{-\infty} = 1/\infty \to 0$. Would it then be true that $0_{-\infty} = 0/\infty \to \infty$? If this so, then $x_{-\infty} = x/\infty \to 0$ ($\infty \neq x \neq 0$), but is not itself reciprocal. The statement $0_{-\infty} = 0/\infty \to \infty$ has interesting side effects also. At zero the quanta ceases to exist, and therein lay another holistic, hence the approach to infinite. This leads to Axiom 20. Finally, the last statement on the Holistic (it is its own antithesis) is logical because Transcendental Metaphysical Reality constitutes all three measurable conditions (Axiom 5).

## Logical Syllogism (Presentation Approach)

Our main purpose here is to examine the systematic way in which people effectively exchange information. This is critical because the process helps to solve problems. In this section we will examine presentations in general (and the rules apply in writing also), the structure of presentations (logical syllogism, a.k.a. the five paragraph theme), the elements of argument, and provide an example presentation that covers almost exactly the same materials using a syllogistic/thematic approach.

### Presentation Issues

Scripts—While a script may be very helpful, never be a script drone. Use a script to formulate and practice. Unless you are acting, do not memorize the script. Never read your script to the audience.

Naturalness—Effective speaking and acting are natural. The speaker must feel memorized script so its presentation will contain those feelings as inflections of tone, gestures and other body language. Without these, the representation sounds rehearsed.

Succinctness—Deliver the information necessary to make your point. Presentation aids must be simple and not distract from the content. Busy charts and diagrams are difficult to follow. Long bodies of text are also. Divide up the information and slowly break the audience in on the big picture rather than inflict it all at once in one diagram or statement. Colors, pictures and sounds should accentuate information and not distract.

Timeliness—Timing is more than just fitting into a speaking schedule. The length of a presentation depends on many factors, including the content and the method of presentation. You may be able to captivate an audience for hours on a subject you fill with energy and enthusiasm. Likewise you may be forced to provide a few raw facts and cut the presentation to a few boring minutes. Keep in mind the attention span of the audience, regardless of the time limitations given to your presentation. Children have very short attention spans for speeches (sometimes less than a few minutes) while adults may last for hours. In reverse, adults will bore more quickly of repetitive physical interactions, while a child will repeat the same action continuously and tirelessly for hours. A normal lecture, for example, has an ideal time of 50 minutes for an adult audience. Consider who the audience is, their interest in the topic, your interest in the topic, your ability to enliven the topic with enthusiasm, then fit what you can into the time given to deliver the presentation.

Structure—The structure of your speech may be more important than the content. The structure will help define the content in a manner the audience can easily comprehend. The less interaction/feedback you have from your audience, the more important the structure. In a completely interactive environment you can literally get away with setting some objectives, practice argument scenarios, set a beginning point and proceed without further structure. This method is much more difficult and is appropriate for smaller audiences. It requires a firm mastery of structured debate/presentation as the speaker must be able to think quickly, formulate and structure arguments in response to any scenario that arises in the presentation. To make matters worse, the unstructured presentation requires that to meet the objectives the speaker must retain them clearly no matter what deviations arise.

## *Thematic Presentation Structure*

### Introduction

The following breakdown goes sentence by sentence through a simple five-paragraph theme. The outline is intended for simplicity. In other words students just learning the five paragraph theme should focus on simple sentences and ideas rather than long and ambiguous sentences. Long and ambiguous sentences in thesis statements and the introduction require greater amounts of information to support them. They also cause the writer to put details in where they do not belong. Concision is highly recommended for beginners. As the student becomes more fluent in the methodology, then this can be expanded to a larger format.

We note that each of the following five paragraphs has five sentences. These sentences may be broken down into the following three categories:

1. Thesis (topic) statement—This is a position statement, a claim of being. Generally it contains two major parts: the topic and an adjective (e.g. The sky is blue). The adjective is the claim, which the rest of the paragraph (or paper if it is the general thesis statement) develops and establishes as fact. It is wise to keep the thesis statement to a singular adjective; otherwise each adjective must be proved. An easy question to answer to establish a thesis statement is: "What word or phrase best describes your feelings about the topic?"

2. Subtopic (descriptive) statement—Each paragraph contains a minimum of three subtopical sentences, which briefly describe specific qualities of the paragraph's thesis statement. Here the question being answered is: "What are the major groups of characteristics of the topic?" or "What specific evidence proves the claim?"

3. Transition statement—Each paragraph ends with a sentence that relates the qualities described in the subtopic statements to the adjective

```
                              GTS
                    ┌──────────┼──────────┐
                   GT1        GT2        GT3
                    └──────────┼──────────┘
                              GTC
        ┌─────────────────────┼─────────────────────┐
       T1                     T2                     T3
  ┌─────┼─────┐         ┌─────┼─────┐         ┌─────┼─────┐
 E1A   E1B   E1C       E2A   E2B   E2C       E3A   E3B   E3C
  │     │     │         │     │     │         │     │     │
 E1A   E1B   E1C       E2A   E2B   E2C       E3A   E3B   E3C
  └─────┼─────┘         └─────┼─────┘         └─────┼─────┘
       TS1                   TS2                   TS3
        └─────────────────────┼─────────────────────┘
                              GS
                    ┌──────────┼──────────┐
                   CT1        CT2        CT3
                    └──────────┼──────────┘
                              GC
```

| | |
|---|---|
| **T = Topic / Thesis** | **G = General** |
| **TS = Transition Statement** | **E = Evidence** |
| **S = Statement** | **C = Conclusion** |

of the thesis statement. Each transition basically answers one question: "What is the relationship between the subtopics (description) and the position (adjective) of the topic?"

## First Paragraph—Introduction

The introductory paragraph establishes what will be argued (the topic and position) and the qualities that will be used to establish the argument. The greater the simplicity the better for beginners. Absolutely no specific details go into this paragraph. In other words don't be descriptive, merely identify the topic and it's adjective in one sentence, the subtopics in separate sentences, and the relationship between these subtopics and the claim (adjective).

Sentence 1—Thesis—This is the general thesis of the paper, stating the topic and an adjective that summarizes a position or feeling about the topic.

Sentences 2-4—Subtopics—One sentence for each of three (minimum) qualities, which comprise the general topic of the paper. Each sentence topic here (the active noun of the sentence) becomes the subject of a paragraph in the body of the paper.

Sentence 5—Transition—One sentence relating the subtopics of sentences 2-4 with the claim (adjective) of sentence 1.

## Second through Fourth Paragraphs—Body

Each of these paragraphs is identical in structure and description, though each will contain separate topics and details describing the topics. These are the only paragraphs in the paper where specific details are provided.

Sentence 1—Topic Statement—Take the subtopics of sentences 2-4 of the first paragraphs and write position statements about them in order. Each of these position statements will contain a subtopic from the introductory paragraph and an adjective summarizing a position or feeling about that subtopic. These three statements will be the thesis statements of paragraph 2-4 respectively.

Sentences 2-4—Description—Break down the thesis statement of the paragraph into three parts (minimum) and describe each separately in at least one sentence (beginners should stick to a single sentence).

Sentence 5—Transition—One sentence relating the descriptive sentences 2-4 with the claim (adjective) of sentence 1.

## Fifth Paragraph—Conclusion

The purpose of this paragraph is to finalize and summarize the paper. Each of the first four sentences is derived from the transitions of the first four paragraphs in order. This does not mean repeating the transitions from those paragraphs. Instead we look at each transition and ask the question: "What does this mean to the topic?" The answer to this will provide a meaningful adjective. The adjective does not have to agree with the claims of the respective paragraphs, but must agree with the evidence and transition provided.

Sentence 1—Final Claim—The adjective will be the final claim of the paper, and may in fact be the same as the thesis statement. The adjective has now been thought through more thoroughly because of the evidence and descriptions provided in paragraphs 2-4, and may become more specific, even contradicting the thesis.

Sentences 2-4—The adjective will become a topic in the conclusive transition. Again, these adjectives may be very similar to those in their respective paragraphs. They may also have changed because of the evidence, and may be better refined.

Sentence 5—Conclusive Transition—Tie the adjective topics of sentences 2-4 with the adjective of the first sentence to either support or condemn the thesis. If the thesis is condemned, this may affect the verbiage of the first sentence of this paragraph (hence altering the adjective of this paragraph's thesis statement).

## Common Errors

Do not begin a five-paragraph theme with a question. While this may work in an eclectic writing style, it fails in the five-paragraph theme. Instead of writing a question for the thesis, answer the question. The answer is your position and what you will find evidence to support or condemn. Transitions are not mini-conclusions. Looking on transitions as mini-conclusions is misleading. The associated mistake with this is having the transitions repeated verbatim in the conclusion. While the transition does conclude the paragraph, it merely summarizes it so the audience has a feeling of wholeness. It acts like the last line in a haiku poem by tying the first statement with the distinctly separate statements that follow. As such the writer should be cautioned to avoid using the adjective of the thesis (claim) in the body of the paragraph. The adjective is included with the subtopics (and often the general topic) in the transition.

### The Creating Process

Introduction—Formulating a presentation is exactly like writing a paper. The writing process remains fundamentally the same, with the exception being that visuals (textual, graphical and animated) audio materials, handouts, and props, not to mention interactive discussions, question and answer periods, etc. may all be included in the product. The writing process consists of the following elements:

Discovering/Impulse—Hodges' makes no reference to this most fundamental (and perhaps obvious) stage. This is perhaps the most creative part of the entire process because here you identify what it is you will present. Borrowing in part from John Dewey's philosophy of creativity and art, we can say that this creative impulse arises from an experience in which one becomes inspired to relate unlike things, and hence to create and express. In some instances this may be very unglamorous (e.g. your boss gives you a project and tells you to present given information at a meeting). No matter where it comes from, the initial idea of the presentation must arise before anything else can occur. This is not to say, however, that you immediately know your thesis. You at least know the major topic of which you wish to express.

Planning—In the creative process, this is where you decide on how you will present the materials. At this point you must identify your audience, the setting, your available resources, your purpose, the time available, etc. This information will outline specifically what dimensions of your topic to address.

Drafting—Again an under-rated step in the process, because it also includes the gathering of information resources, compiling raw data, making claims about the data, extracting evidence, substantiating with warrants (sources of the evidence), summarizing the relationship between the evidence and claims, and organizing everything in a meaningful and sequential manner.

Proofreading—Hodges' places this step last in the list, when it is an on-going process beginning with the first draft. Proofreading may coincide with editing, but is fundamentally different. Proofreading involves reading through the entire draft from beginning to end to check for coherence, clarity, and that the materials follow a logical sequence that fills the objectives of the expression. In other words the fundamental objective of proofreading is in the questions "Does it make sense?" and "Does it say what was intended to be said?" It is often wise to have a third party proofread your document who knows nothing about the subject. The reason is that the third party will hold the author accountable for anything that is less than perfectly clear, and force the author into the "beginner's mind." When creating an expression it is easy to forget that our first purpose is to inform our audience about the experience of our perspective, and that they have not shared the experience until now. Our expression becomes an artificial experience. If the audience shared in the same experience previously, then what is the point in boring them with doing it again? If not, then we must be mindful that our terminology and references are such that every member in the audience can relate. Otherwise the author becomes the sole audience to appreciate the expression and it fails.

Editing—This is a professional stage of the writing process in which the document is reviewed for its style, grammar, syntax, spelling, punctuation, form, etc. Any common person can easily distinguish between a professional and amateur expression, even if they do not know what exactly the distinctions are. The professional has a firm grasp of the distinction from research, education, and personal experience. The professional editor easily identifies the tiniest details that make the expression less than professional. As a consequence you must make yourself a professional editor by experiencing the field, reading and referencing appropriate and current resources, and practicing your methods of expressing. Ask yourself what methods have worked best for what methods. Why? How can you use these same methods or modify them to fit your needs?

Worksheet 3—System Architectures
Unit 4—Logic

Revising—This is an on-going process that occurs following every cycle of proofreading and editing until the document has reached a final and effective form. Note that the easiest way to enter editing and proofreading corrections is to begin at the end of the document and work your way to the beginning. This way you can easily find the location of corrections. If you begin at the start, then the corrections will shift the rest of the materials and make it difficult to find where future corrections go.

Hodges' Harbrace College Handbook (11th ed, 1990, p 576) incorrectly states there is no fixed order to these. The above order is correct. The authors perhaps are confused between Writing Process and Writing Order. Writing Order depends largely on the skills of the writer and the knowledge of the subject. The five paragraph theme presented in the previous section negates the need for skill and enables the writer to experience an unknown topic, explore its elements, and derive a conclusion. If the author knows a lot about the subject, then writing the introductory paragraph is fairly simple. If not, then the introductory paragraph is put last. An experienced orator who is familiar with the topic being discussed can instantly use the above system to formulate an impromptu argument. We see this very commonly in political debates.

## Elements of Argument

### Introduction

The structure of argument has evolved from Aristotle's logos (logic or structure), pathos (feeling), ethos (value) to Hegel's thesis (claim), antithesis (what is not the claim), synthesis (outcome or conclusion resulting from combining the thesis and antithesis) to the current form of claim (position), support (evidence), warrant (source). The thematic approach combines the elements of argument with the scientific methodology of Sir Francis Bacon as applied to writing: Problem, Theoretical Framework, Methods, Observations, Conclusion; or in short: Introduction, Body, Conclusion. Though the short definitions for quick reference provided in this text are helpful for quick reference, in-depth definitions are more expository and concrete.

|  | Structure | Voice | Purpose |  |
|---|---|---|---|---|
| Logos |  |  |  |  |
| Pathos |  |  |  | Degree Of |
| Ethos |  |  |  | Application |

### Aristotle

Logos—A style of writing, in which the elements of a subject are put into a specific viewpoint. The elements are then given order, purpose, and understanding. This is done to explain fundamental relationships within a set of facts. Logos has distinct functions in all documents. This is an inherent feature of logical syllogism, the five paragraph theme. Information is gathered, given order, and presented to support a specific thesis. It is important that you, as a writer, not neglect ethos and pathos, and adhere entirely to logos. Be mindful of which is dominant in each writing case. Certainly logos is fundamental to holding any argument together.

Pathos—A writing style in which the writer is trying to arouse a deep emotion. This emotion is usually tender, such as passion, compassion, etc. It can also be a negative appeal, which is a less effective style. Pathos is part of the persuasive element of every argument. The process of arguing is going to be logos. Ethos is most likely what is addressed in the argument. The voice you will use to address the ethos will be pathos.

Ethos—A style of writing in which values are identified. Ethos gives an argument value, especially moral or ethical value. Because of the attachment with values, especially those that can be defined as fitting a specific and definable population (which is definitive of moral and ethical, where moral is a limited population, and ethical is an universal population), ethos is perhaps strongest motivator as the second persuasive element of every argument.

### Hegel

Thesis—Hegel's thesis is slightly different from the one we use here, but the concept is important. Essentially his thesis is a statement of "is-ness" identifying an object and what constitutes or defines that object. In research this thesis is often called hypothetical, which is based upon the known components of an object.

Antithesis—The antithesis is the opposite of the thesis. Here you take the components defining the thesis object and restate them as negatives (e.g. what we know a thing is not). In research we typically use the term null hypothesis, which defines the testable components of the research. You test the null hypothesis because it will validate the conditions outlined in the hypothesis.

Synthesis—The combination of observations in the thesis and antithesis to illustrate an even bigger (more holistic) picture. In other words, the process of showing how the object being investigated/argued interacts with other objects of unlike definition. If our thesis is on bread, then our antithesis would necessarily be non-bread items, such as meat, preserves, butter, etc. Our resulting synthesis combines these unlike objects to illustrate that we can interact these unlike things and consequently get sandwiches, toast, etc.

## Contemporary

Claim—Represents what you are trying to prove or say. It is a small conclusion in a sense, but it may be more like a leading hypothesis. It tells your audience what issue you are going to address (it is sometimes referred to as a hook, because the audience identifies themselves as interested or not interested by what it says, and how it is written). Every paper should start with a general claim. This claim is commonly called a thesis statement. I will not limit the scope of this to a thesis sentence because that is misleading. Depending on the scope of the document, the thesis statement can be as small as a sentence, or as large as an introduction. Whatever you assert in your thesis statement, you must substantiate in the body of your paper-preferably in the order they are presented in the introduction.

Support—The evidence you provide. It should appeal to the needs, expectations and values of your audience in order to substantiate your claim. A good format to follow is to make your claim first, maintaining a logical hierarchy of order as illustrated above, and then follow with supporting evidence. Evidence is facts, not opinions or what you think are facts (though some expert opinions are considered factual enough for use in argument--these are either quoted or paraphrased and cited). If you cannot find your evidence documented by a valid source, then avoid using it. This is not to say that you have to find documentation on items of extreme common knowledge. For example, you can say the sky is blue. Though some small sample of the population may disagree, it is widely accepted and documented. However, you cannot say tat Christopher Columbus discovered America in 1492 without being subject to scrutiny for fallacy. Many historians will argue to the death on this. They will argue that the American Indians (Amerands) came first, then the Norwegians, Dutch, and finally Columbus. Some even claim that an Irishman came before Columbus, and that the Portuguese came close. As a matter of fact, Columbus never reached the continent, and could not even navigate well enough to return to the same island he discovered in the first place. So you have to be careful about what is common knowledge and what is common myth.

Warrant—Gives authenticity to the support. There are two forms of warrants, the expressed and unexpressed warrants. In the expressed warrant a particular authority or group of authorities is mentioned as having made a conclusion. This conclusion is the evidence you provide. An unexpressed warrant is better used with items of common knowledge. In these you don't need to say who the authority is that made the conclusion. Most of us would be able to say that most wheels are round. If we were to discuss triangular wheels, which do exist, we would have to cite an authority on that type of wheel. If you don't do this, the reader is put in a situation where they can be doubtful of your assertions. If a conclusion or opinion seems to be widely shared in your research, then unless you quote someone an expressed warrant (citation) is not necessary. It may be helpful though, for researchers, if you made a footnote or parenthetical remark listing some of the people you could have cited. When writing fiction, and especially science fiction and fantasy, we tend not to express our warrants. It is unwise for an author to be too outrageous in claims and supports, even in fiction. If they are, the audience will have a hard time relating to the story.

## Scientific

The scientific method has undergone many changes since Sir Francis Bacon, using syllogism to report the exploration of a topic. The format described here is used for technical research including theses and dissertations. Sections may migrate occasionally or even be forgotten, while others may be added to further map the process. The key to the scientific model is to create a report such that another researcher can follow the same process and achieve the same results. On the whole the following outline is fairly consistent, and must be to insure findings are easily validated, replicated and expressed.

| Chapter | Section | Description |
|---|---|---|
| Introduction/ Problem | Statement of the Problem | Identifies the issue being researched. |
| | Purpose | States the motive for conducting the research. |
| | Significance | States why the research is important. |
| | Limitations | Gives a scope to the research (e.g. what it can be applied to externally). |
| | Delimitations | States internal factors that could influence the research. |
| Theoretical Framework | Literature Review | Examines what other researchers have found, and their methods of achieving results. |
| | Hypothesis | An educated guess as to the outcome of the research; a statement of what a thing may be. |
| | Null-Hypothesis | A statement of what is not present, and by the absence of that quality the existence of the hypothesis is proven (Cicero's "Exception proves the rule"). |
| Methodology | Nature | Statement defining the type of research being conducted: quantitative, qualitative, exploratory, descriptive, primary, secondary, historical, triangulated, etc. |
| | Method | What method is employed: experimental, quasi-experimental, survey, obtrusive or non-obtrusive observation, etc.? Define the method being employed. If the subjects are obtrusively observed, what is done to return normalcy (e.g. post-test counseling)? |
| | Population | What defines the whole population to whom your study applies? |
| | Sampling Method | How will you determine who will be studied of the population. |
| | Statistical Methods | What numeric methods (if any) will you use to insure that your findings are meaningful and representative of the entire population? |
| Observations | Appropriate Headings | Headings break down aspects of the observations to help guide the reader. This chapter is exclusively raw data but may also contain "gut feelings" clearly identified by the researcher while the observations occurred. |
| Conclusion | Meaning | What do all the observations mean? How do they apply to what? |
| | New Issues | What new questions are asked as a consequence? If there was a problem with the design, how would you do it better next time? |
| | Conclusion | Was the hypothesis supported or discarded? What is left? What is now known that was not before? What is next? |

**_Thematic Presentation Example_**

The following is a PowerPoint presentation using syllogism to discuss syllogism.

---

**POWERPOINT 97**

Thematic Presentation
Procedures

© 1999 by George Yool

**1**

---

## Thematic Presentation Procedures

Introduction
Thematic presentations are easy to create and to follow.

- Presentation Issues
- Thematic Structure
- Elements of Argument
- The Creating Process
- Writing Order

We will explore these topics to show how to easily create thematic presentations.

**2**

---

## Presentation Issues

Introduction
The audience is the most important element of your presentation.

- Scripts
- Naturalness
- Professionalism
- Succinctness
- Timeliness
- Structure

Careful attention to these elements means being mindful of your audience.

**3**

---

## Scripts

Scripts can help and hinder your presentation.

| Hindrances | Helps |
|---|---|
| •Droning—not having emotion<br>•Reading directly—so can the audience<br>•Memorizing—sounds rehearsed Abstract terms—speaks over audience | •Preparation—establish perspective<br>•Formulate—concepts, examples, order<br>•Practice—timing and voice Vernacular—speaks to audience |

Find a useful balance in your use of scripts.

**4**

---

## Naturalness

Effective speaking and acting are natural.

If you must memorize, include feelings as:

- inflections of tone
- gestures
- other body language

Without feelings, the presentation sounds rehearsed and unnatural.

**5**

---

## Professionalism

Professionalism takes practice and skill.

- Know the facts
- Appreciate different viewpoints
- Never fill time
- Be confident but not arrogant
- Never speak at or down to the audience

Professionalism gives your speech authority.

**6**

---

## Succinctness

Deliver the information necessary to make your point.

- Keep presentation aids simple:
- Do not distract from the content
- Busy charts and diagrams are difficult
- Long bodies of text are difficult
- Divide the big picture and feed in pieces

Aids must accentuate information, not distract from it.

7

## Timeliness

Timing depends on content and method of presentation.

Longer Presentation
- Fill with energy and enthusiasm
- Interactive and experiential
- Older Audience (adults typically 50 minutes)
- Professionals

Shorter Presentation
- Raw facts
- Younger audience (children—a few minutes)
- Uninterested audience
- Non-professionals

8

## Consider

- who the audience is
- their interest in the topic
- your interest in the topic
- your ability to enliven the topic with enthusiasm
- how interactive the presentation
- fit what you can into the time given

The audience, your topic and your skills determine timing.

9

## Structure

Audience comprehension of your presentation
depends on interactivity.

Completely Interactive Requires:
- smaller audiences
- firm mastery of debate & topic
- quick thinking
- always retain objectives

Method:
- set objectives
- practice argument scenarios
- ask the audience questions
- counter their responses

10

## Non-Interactive

Requires:
- Strict structure
- Complete Simplicity

Method:
- Establish one position
- Present syllogistically

Interactivity defines the structure necessary to insure
audience comprehension.

11

## Presentation Issues
### (Conclusion)

Careful attention to presentation issues means being mindful of
your audience.

- Use scripts with caution
- Put feeling into your presentation
- Have professional authority
- Use helpful and simple presentation aids
- Meter time to suite your skills, topic and audience
- Balance interactivity with presentation structure

These tips balance your presentation so your audience will
appreciate, listen and understand.

12

## Thematic Structure
### (Logical Syllogism)

Introduction
Thematic presentations are easily created, delivered and comprehended.

- Statement types
- General construction
- Common errors

Ability to use the correct statements in a logical sequence prevents awkwardness and other errors.

13

## Statement Types

Statements consist of everything from sentences to sections in a volume.

- Logical syllogism uses three statement types:
- Thesis Statement
- Descriptive/Evidentiary Statement
- Transition Statement

14

## Qualities of Statements

Statement types always:

- Follow the same order
- Contain the same elements
- Sequentially build up from the sentence

The sequence of sentence, paragraph and larger statements make writing and comprehension easy.

15

## Thesis Statement

Thesis statements are easy to write.

- They state the topic or subtopic
- They present a feeling about the topic (adjective)
- Answer: "What sentence tells the topic and a feeling about it?"
- Establish a claim or position

These details and the example given here show thesis statements are easy to write.

16

## Descriptive/Evidentiary Statement

Evidentiary statements are the body and details supporting the claim.

- Always have at least three details
- Be specific with the evidence
- Never distract from the local claim
- Many details justify separate claims

Three specific details are sufficient to establish a simple claim.

17

## Transition Statement

Transitions tie the evidence with the claim like the last line of a haiku poem.

- Creates unity among the statements
- Relates the details to the adjective
- Answers: "What is the relationship between the evidence (description) and the position (adjective) of the topic?"

Transitions say the thought is complete so the audience can move forward to the next idea/argument.

18

## General Construction

Syllogism similarly defines the overall structure of the document/presentation.

- Introduction
- Body (3 statements/paragraphs)
- Conclusion

These, in conjunction with the sequence of statements within them, constitute the five-paragraph theme.

19

## First Paragraph—Introduction

The introduction gives order to the entire document.

- Establishes the topic and position
- Introduces qualities used to support position
- No specific details in this paragraph
- Ties subtopics with topic position (transition)

The qualities become the rank order in which subtopics will be individually established.

20

## Second through Fourth Paragraphs—Body

The body follows the order of subtopics provided in the introduction.

- Establishes the position of the subtopic
- Provides specific evidence
- Ties evidence with subtopic position (transition)

Each paragraph in the body is a separate argument from the thesis and specific to the subtopic.

21

## Fifth Paragraph—Conclusion

The conclusion transforms the transitions in order into statements of fact.

- Affirms or denies the topic position
- Provides synthesis of details (subtopics)
- Ties synthesis of details with position

By restating the transitions as facts, the conclusion provides a final synopsis of the argument.

22

## Thematic Model

```
                    GTS
            GT1   GT2   GT3
                    GTC
   T1              T2              T3
E1A E1B E1C    E2A E2B E2C    E3A E3B E3C
E1A E1B E1C    E2A E2B E2C    E3A E3B E3C
   TS1            TS2            TS3
                    GS
            CT1   CT2   CT3
                    GC
```

T = Topic / Thesis          G = General
TS = Transition Statement   E = Evidence
S = Statement               C = Conclusion

23

## Common Errors

In spite of the simplicity of syllogism, there remain many misconceptions.

- Never begin with a question
- Answer the question (your thesis)
- Transitions are not mini-conclusions
- Do not repeat transitions verbatim in the conclusion
- Avoid using the adjective of the thesis (claim) in the body of the paragraph
- Never say "In conclusion..." or similar verbiage
- Never begin any sentence with but, and, or, then, however, etc.

Avoiding these common errors will help make your presentation/document look more professional.

24

## Thematic Structure
### (Conclusion)

Use of syllogism prevents awkwardness of expressed communications.

Be mindful of statement sequence and content:
- Thesis/Claim—topic (subtopic) and position (adjective)
- Evidence—At least three specific details
- Transition/Synthesis—tie evidence to claim

25

## Thematic Structure
### (Conclusion Continued)

The Five Paragraph Theme gives general structure:

- Introduction—qualities give order of subtopics
- Body—details establish subtopic positions
- Conclusion—converts transitions into final statements of fact
- Avoid common errors to retain professional authority

Syllogism balances statements, paragraphs and content for effective communication.

26

## Elements of Argument

Introduction

The elements of argument apply to any communication.
Their creators provide methods of:

| Source | Provides Methods of: |
|---|---|
| Aristotle | 1. Style  2. Presentation |
| Hegel | 3. Problem Solving |
| Contemporary | 4. Validation |
| Scientific (Sir Francis Bacon) | 5. Reporting |

Using the methods provided in these elements make for easy and consistent communications.

27

## Aristotle

Aristotle defines elements for methods of style and presentation.

Style consists of:
- Logos—a specific viewpoint (logic)
- Pathos—use of emotions (experience)
- Ethos—use of values (measurement)

Presentation consists of:
- Structure—consistent methods
- Voice—tone and word choice
- Purpose—meaning, raison d'etre

28

## Balancing Style and Presentation Elements

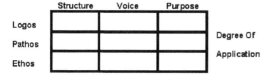

By balancing style and presentation methods we establish ourselves as an authority and motivate the audience to action.

29

## Hegel

Hegel defined the elements of problem solving using inductive reasoning.

- Thesis—define the process
- Antithesis—define what is not the process
- Synthesis—combine to find bigger process

By looking at smaller parts, Hegel's method tells us about the big picture.

30

## Contemporary

Contemporary speakers emphasize methods to assure internal validity of an argument.

- Claim—statement of topic and position
- Support—evidence substantiating position
- Warrant—authoritative sources of support

By balancing claims with warranted evidence, contemporary speakers make their arguments are more valid.

31

## Scientific

The scientific model uses syllogism to report the exploration of a topic.

- Problem—the topic and what is being explored
- Theoretical Framework—what the literature says
- Method—sequence of how information is gathered
- Observation—describe the new information
- Conclusion—synthesize old and new to solve problem

The scientific model makes findings easy to validate, replicate and express.

32

## Elements of Argument

Conclusion
The elements of argument provide methods for easy and consistent communications.

- Style and presentation establish authority and motivate
- Examining the parts describes the whole problem
- Balance of claims with warranted evidence provides internal validity
- The scientific reporting model provides external validity

The elements of style give authenticity and inspiration to any communication.

33

## The Creating Process

The creative process follows a simple order, not to be confused with writing order.
- Discovery/Impulse— what it is you will present
- Planning—how you will present the materials
- Drafting—gathering facts and putting them in order
- Proofreading—check for coherence, clarity, and sequence
- Editing—review style, grammar, syntax, spelling, punctuation, form, etc.
- Revising—make corrections beginning at the end of the document

An experienced orator can instantly use this system to formulate an impromptu argument.

34

## Writing Order

Writing Order depends largely on the skills of the writer and the knowledge of the subject.

- Little knowledge or experience:
- Write body, introduction then conclusion
- A lot of knowledge and experience:
- Write introduction, body then conclusion

Syllogism is permissive of inexperience, allowing easy exploration of new topics, their elements and deriving conclusions.

35

## Thematic Presentation Procedures
### (Conclusion)

We explored several topics to show how to easily create thematic presentations.

- Be mindful of presentation issues
- Use syllogism to balance your argument
- Use argument to inspire and authenticate
- Develop impromptu/spontaneous skills
- Explore new topics, their elements and derive conclusions

Syllogism is the ultimate simple way for anyone to improve their communication skills and express complex ideas to any audience.

36

# Flowcharting

## *Symbols*

Flowcharts are graphical representations of step-by-step processes describing how to perform a specific function. This table illustrates the symbols and their meanings.

| | | | | | |
|---|---|---|---|---|---|
| Alternate Process | Alternate Process | Another process that provides the same results as the primary process. | Annotation | Annotation | A brief note to help the reader understand a chart item or series of symbols better. |
| Collate | Collate | Keeping a series together in multiple copies (e.g. printing the entire document for each copy rather than printing all copies of each page at the same time). | Delay | Delay | Typically used to make one process wait while another occurs (e.g. waiting for water to boil). |
| Decision | IF | Decisions typically provide true and false choices which can be chained together for more complex decisions, which are shown by having more than two extruding arrows. | | | |
| Direct Access Storage | Direct Access Storage | Any data stored on a fixed media such as RAM, ROM, and Hard Disk. | Display | Display | Indicates data being shown on the CRT (monitor). |
| Document | Document | Indicates a file (or less typically but equally useful with databases, a record). | Magnetic Disk Storage | Magnetic Disk Storage | Data stored on floppy disk. |
| Directional Arrow | | Indicates the direction the process is flowing. Note that a double arrow is almost never used. | Extract | Extract | To take a sample (less than the population) of information or separate information into multiple items. |
| Input and Output | Input / Output | More typically used for input than output (due to other available output symbols). Typically this symbol contains an input question. | Internal Connector | | Typically contains a letter and appears at least twice. The internal connector connects to or more points within a chart (only one of which will have an arrow pointing away from it). |
| Internal Storage | Internal Storage | Data stored and used within the process. When used, always indicates the process is an object. Note: if the data is not internal, then it should be identified as public with indication as to the source. | Manual Input | Manual Input | As the label suggests, this is any operator/human executed event such as typing information. |
| Manual Operation | Manual Operation | As with the manual input, a manual operation is performed by the operator and not by the program itself. | Merge | Merge | To combine multiple sources of information into one item. |

| Multiple Documents | Multiple Documents | A group of related files (or less commonly a group of related records in a data base). | Off-Chart Connector | Off-Chart Connection | Off-chart connections contain a name, typically the name of another process (object). |
| Or | OR | Used to signify parallel solutions that may depend on the information provided. | Predefined Process | Predefined Process | Uses a stored (e.g. public) process (such as from the Main( ) object), perhaps indicating an off-chart connection to a part of another object. |
| Preparation | Preparation | Collecting input data in a useable format. | Sequential Data Storage | Sequential Data Storage | Data stored on tape or in a definable sequence (order). |
| Process | Process | Any operation where input is converted to output, such as a mathematical formula. | Sort | Sort | Puts data into a sequential order. Be sure to indicate if the sort is in reverse order and, if applicable, the criteria of the sort. |
| Stored Data | Stored Data | Raw data stored in the specified manner. | Summing Junction | ⊗ | The point at which the data from multiple sources is brought together. |
| Terminator | Begin() End | All charts begin with a terminator. Charts that do not end in a terminator form endless loops. | | | |

## Flowchart Creation

This illustration provides a simple example of how a flowchart provides the step-by-step how-to process. To create a flowchart, follow the one below. Note: this chart requires that you have some knowledge of the input, output, or manipulation method. If you have information about the input or output, you must determine the method.

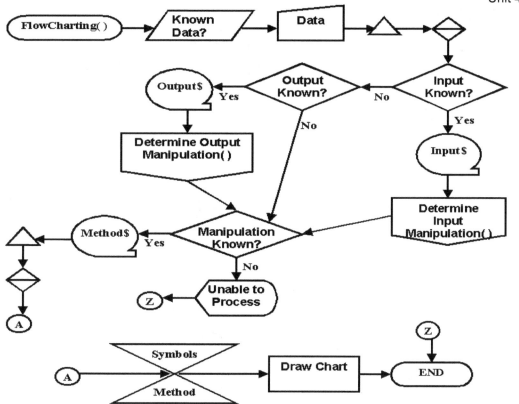

## **Flowcharting Examples**

**Boiling Water**

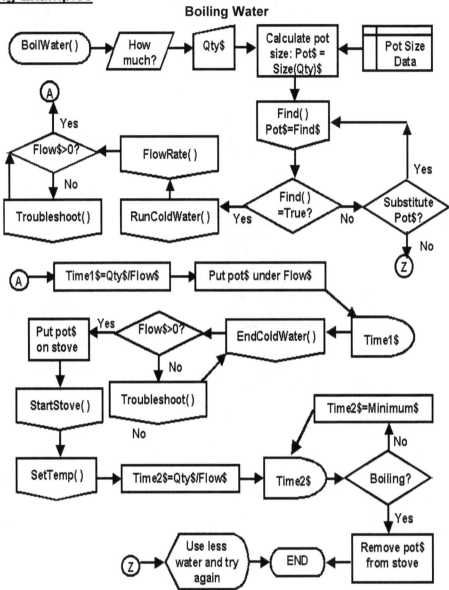

**Putting a Cap on a Pen**

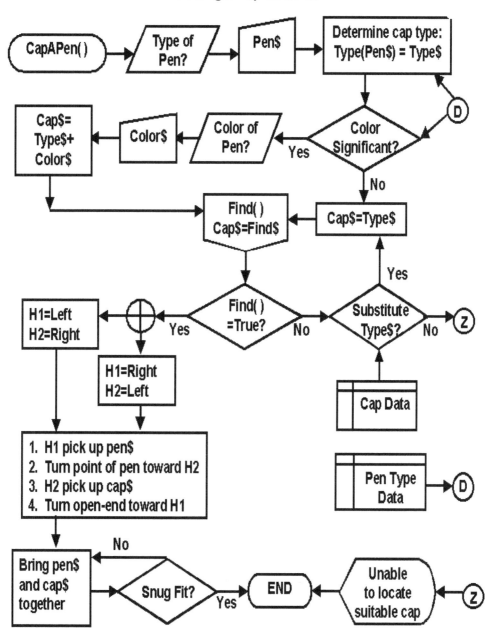

## Solving a Heuristic

A heuristic is slightly different from an algorithm. Algorithms are expected to provide exacting results. Heuristics are only expected to give calculated guesses. Fundamentally they are identical on the surface. Where they differ is the exactitude. When might you need a heuristic? Consider the famous traveling salesman problem. Basically the story goes this way: the salesman has N points to visit. He wants to travel as little distance as possible, and preferably not have to backtrack. What is his best route? If the salesman is a machine, and the points don't care either, you don't have to worry about how he feels about the points, or when they would like to see him. In such a case you use an algorithm. Since the salesman and the customers do care, you must devise a heuristic, which will not necessarily work for other salesmen, nor will it work if someone new moves into the neighborhood.

## Polyhedron Problem

Polyhedrons are three-dimensional figures, such as cubes, pyramids, spheres, etc. We will focus on polyhedrons constructed of straight lines, particularly those known as the regular polyhedrons. Our purpose is to learn a little more about both the regular polyhedrons and others that are similar. Euler recognized that polyhedrons have relationships between their faces, edges and vertices ($E=F+V-2$) and identified five shapes as regular. There is only one problem with Euler's model: it alone cannot be used to prove or disprove the existence of other regular polyhedrons because we must have two variables to calculate the third.

## Polyhedron Solution

The solution must allow for the calculation of the other variables based on only one of these, namely the number of faces. We must add two variables: the number of sides on one face (S) and the number of edges joining at each vertice (J). After further observation we are able to expand our table as follows:

| Name | Faces (F) | Edges (E) | Vertices (V) | Sides (S) | Joints (J) |
|---|---|---|---|---|---|
| Tetrahedron | 4 | 6 | 4 | 3 | 3 |
| Hexahedron | 6 | 12 | 8 | 4 | 3 |
| Octahedron | 8 | 12 | 6 | 3 | 4 |
| Dodecahedron | 12 | 30 | 20 | 5 | 3 |
| Icosahedron | 20 | 30 | 12 | 3 | 5 |

We observe that $E = .5FS$ and $J=FS/V$, and. These are important because we can consider a polyhedron problem a graph problem. As a graph problem we need to know what relationships the significant points have. The significant points for a graph problem are the number of vertices, not the number of faces. We humans are most interested in the faces and finding all instances where our attributes (F, E, V, S, J, etc.) are "legal." All instances of these particular attributes must be positive, real integers.

## Problem

Our problem comes in two heuristic parts: a single variable solution and a test to be sure our primary attributes remain positive, real integers. The first heuristic is to solve for S given only F (see pseudocode on right). In short the algorithm divides 360 by the number of faces, then finds all divisors of 3, 4, and 5 of the result. Then the number of instances are arranged and the middle value (or one on the right) is the number of sides on one face (S). The second is to test all our variables to be sure they are valid. We will expand the pseudocode for the Side problem to explain how you might test for a continuous decimal and add a module to round values up (not down!). We will develop a logical process ensuring our system is not bogged down doing unnecessary calculations by testing the attributes most likely to break first.

```
Pseudocode to Find SIDES
Private Float      variable = 360 / Faces
Private Integer  i = 0
Private Array a[3,2]
IF variable ≠ integer and variable = continuous decimal
        NotPossible ( )
IF variable ≠ integer
        remove decimal from variable
FOR i = 1 TO 3
        Public Integer a[i,1] = (i + 2)
        Public Integer a[i,2] = 0
        WHILE modulus of variable/(i + 2) ≠ 0
                a[i,2]++
                variable /= (i+2)
IF variable ≠ 1 or 2
        NotPossible ( )
Return RoundUp (Median ( ))
```

*A Solution:*

**ComputeS (F)**

*/      This counts the number of times 3, 4, & 5 may be divided into N to generate a, b, & c./*

```
{
private double a=0;
private double b=0;
private double c=0;
private double d=360;

if d%F!=0
{
    d=360000000;
    if d%F!=0
    {
        return 0;
        end;
    }
}
else
{
    N=d/F;
    do
    {
        a=a++;
        N=N/3;
    }
    while N%3==0;
    do
    {
        b=b++;
        N=N/4;
    {
    while N%4==0;
    do
    {
        c=c++;
        N=N/5;
    {
    while N%5==0;
    }
    if a+b+c==0 then return 0;
    else if c>=a+b then S=5;
    else a<=b+c?S=4:S=3;
    endif;
    return S;
    }
}
```

Errors:

use a counting module

use a median module

**Decimal (test)**

```
{
    private integer result2 = test;
```

```
    return result2 == test ? 0 : 1;
}
```

**DetermineE (F,S)**
```
{
    Private float E=.5FS
    Decimal(test=E)==1?E=0:E=E;
    return E;
}
```

**DetermineV (F,S,E)**
```
{
    Private float V=E-F+2
    Decimal(test=V)==1?V=0:V=V;
    return V;
}
```

**DetermineJ (F,S,V)**
```
{
    Private float J=FS/V
    Decimal(test=J)==1?J=0:J=J;
    return J;
}
```

**MainTest (F)**
```
Private Integer S=ComputeS(F);
If S!=0 then
{
    E=DetermineE (F,S);
    If!=0 then
        Private Integer V=DetermineE (F,S);
        If V!=0 then
    If DetermineJ (F,S,V)!=0 then cout << "This one works: F =  " << F
```

## Refining the Heuristic

In our previous examination of the sides per face problem, we used basic variable declarations.  In this example I use a two-dimensional array—one dimension for the number of sides, and the other to store the number of occurrences.  The advantage of using an array like this, is that we can easily adjust the code to allow for more variables without having to rewrite the entire program, as the previous example would require.  This example also gives us insight on how we can solve for a statistical median (the center value of an ordered set).

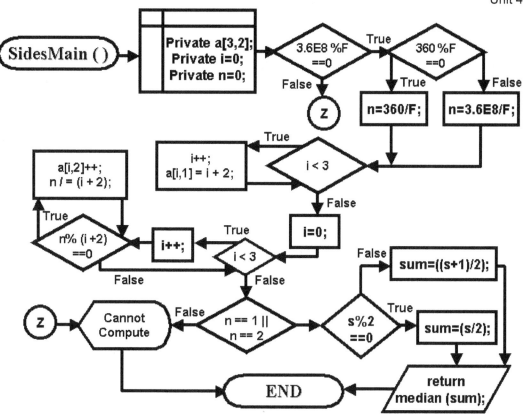

## Solving a Median

A median is a statistical measure of central tendency. In simple terms, when you look at a list of values in order, the median is the value appearing in the middle. Does this sound too easy? Look at the diagram on the right and tell me. This is only the first half of the solution though. Allow me to outline the details of the problem:

1. The user must identify how many items are in the set. This is because the program must know how many variables it must declare.
2. We cannot assume the user will enter the values in order, so we must sort the values.
3. We must verify that replicated values are intentional and not accidental.
4. We want to give the user as many options as possible.

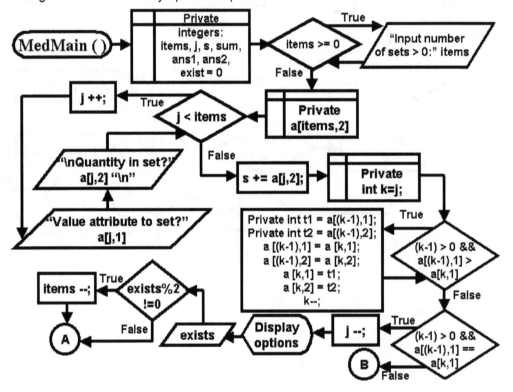

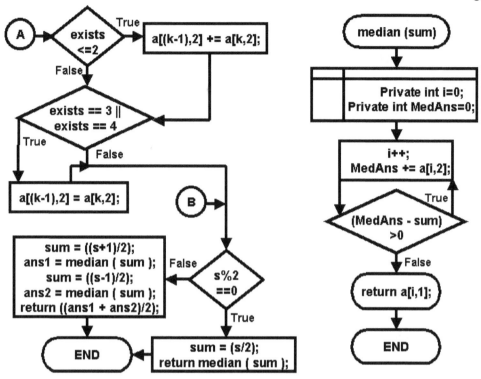

### MedMain ( )

```
//        Declarations
{
Private int items = 0;
Private int j = 0;
Private int s = 0;
Private int sum = 0;
Private int ans1 = 0;
Private int ans2 = 0;
Private int exist = 0;
```

```
//   Input Loop: Number of Sets
While items > =  0
    {
        cout     << "Input number of sets > 0: ";
        cin  >> items;
        cout     << endl;
    }
```

```
//   Input Loop: Set Data
Private a [ items, 2 ];
While j < items
    {
        j++;
        cout     << "Value attributed to set/quality? ";
        cin  >> a [ j, 1 ];
        cout     << "\nQuantity in set? ";
```

```
        cin  >> a [ j, 2 ];
        cout    << endl;
```

```
//      Sum Quantities of Sets
        s + =  a [ j, 2 ];
```

```
//   Sort Set Attributes Ascending
        Private int k = j;
        While (k-1) > 0 && a [ k, 1 ] < a [ (k-1), 1 ]
            {
                Private int t1 = a [ (k-1), 1 ];
                Private int t2 = a [ (k-1), 2 ];
                a [ (k-1), 1 ] =  a [ k, 1 ];
                a [ (k-1), 2 ] =  a [ k, 2 ];
                a [ k, 1 ] =  t1;
                a [ k, 2 ] =  t2;
                k--;
            }
```

```
//   Duplicate Set Handling
        if (k-1) > 0 && a [ k, 1 ] =  =  a [ (k-1), 1 ]
            {
                j--;
                cout    << "This set already exists.  Please choose from the following:\n"
                    << "Add to original set and:\n"
                    << "1.       Reduce number of sets computed.\n"
                    << "2.       Continue without changing number of sets.\n"
                    << "Replace original set and:\n"
                    << "3.       Reduce number of sets computed.\n"
                    << "4.       Continue without changing number of sets.\n"
                    << "Forget this entry and:\n"
                    << "5.       Reduce number of sets computed.\n"
                    << "6.       Continue without changing number of sets.\n";
                cin  >> exists;
                cout    << cls;
```

```
                    //      Duplicate Exists Event Action
                if exists%2 ! =  0
                {
                        items--;
                }
                if exists < =  2
                {
                    a [ (k-1), 2 ] + =  a [ k, 2 ];
                }
                if exists =  =  3 || exists  =  =  4
                {
                    a [ (k-1), 2 ] =  a [ k, 2 ];
                }
            }
        }
```

## //   Median Handling and Results

```
if s%2 = = 0
    {
        sum = (s/2);
        return median(sum);
    }
else
    {
        sum = ((s+1)/2);
        ans1 = median(sum);
        sum = ((s-1)/2);
        ans2 = median(sum);
        return ((ans1+ans2)/2);
    }
break;
```

### *Median ( sum )*

## //   Declarations

```
Private int i = 0;
Private int MedAns = 0;
```

## //   Computational Loop

```
{
    Do
    {
        i++;
        MedAns + =  a [ i, 2 ];
    }
    While (MedAns – sum) > 0
    return a [ i, 1 ];
}
```

# Worksheet 4—Logic

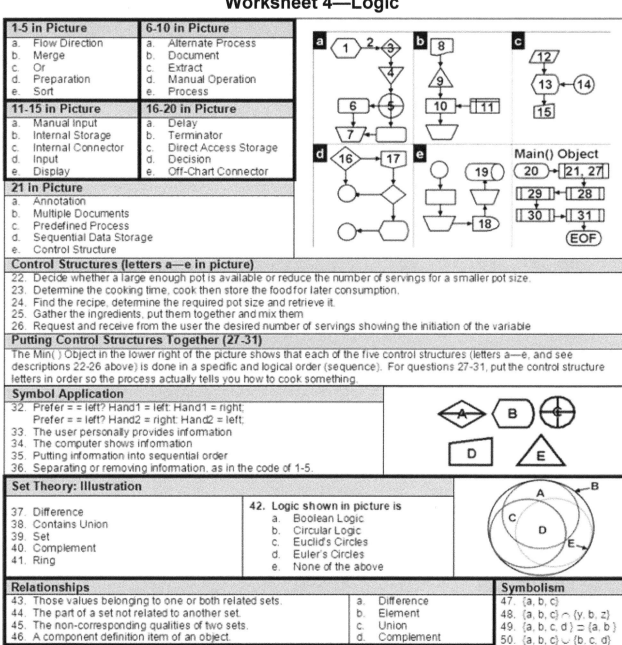

| 1-5 in Picture | 6-10 in Picture |
|---|---|
| a. Flow Direction | a. Alternate Process |
| b. Merge | b. Document |
| c. Or | c. Extract |
| d. Preparation | d. Manual Operation |
| e. Sort | e. Process |

| 11-15 in Picture | 16-20 in Picture |
|---|---|
| a. Manual Input | a. Delay |
| b. Internal Storage | b. Terminator |
| c. Internal Connector | c. Direct Access Storage |
| d. Input | d. Decision |
| e. Display | e. Off-Chart Connector |

**21 in Picture**
a. Annotation
b. Multiple Documents
c. Predefined Process
d. Sequential Data Storage
e. Control Structure

## Control Structures (letters a—e in picture)

22. Decide whether a large enough pot is available or reduce the number of servings for a smaller pot size.
23. Determine the cooking time, cook then store the food for later consumption.
24. Find the recipe, determine the required pot size and retrieve it.
25. Gather the ingredients, put them together and mix them
26. Request and receive from the user the desired number of servings showing the initiation of the variable

## Putting Control Structures Together (27-31)

The Min( ) Object in the lower right of the picture shows that each of the five control structures (letters a—e, and see descriptions 22-26 above) is done in a specific and logical order (sequence). For questions 27-31, put the control structure letters in order so the process actually tells you how to cook something.

## Symbol Application

32. Prefer = = left? Hand1 = left: Hand1 = right;
    Prefer = = left? Hand2 = right: Hand2 = left;
33. The user personally provides information
34. The computer shows information
35. Putting information into sequential order
36. Separating or removing information, as in the code of 1-5.

## Set Theory: Illustration

37. Difference
38. Contains Union
39. Set
40. Complement
41. Ring

**42. Logic shown in picture is**
a. Boolean Logic
b. Circular Logic
c. Euclid's Circles
d. Euler's Circles
e. None of the above

## Relationships

| | | |
|---|---|---|
| 43. Those values belonging to one or both related sets. | a. | Difference |
| 44. The part of a set not related to another set. | b. | Element |
| 45. The non-corresponding qualities of two sets. | c. | Union |
| 46. A component definition item of an object. | d. | Complement |

## Symbolism

47. {a, b, c}
48. {a, b, c} ∩ {y, b, z}
49. {a, b, c, d} ⊃ {a, b }
50. {a, b, c} ∪ {b, c, d}
51. hair ∈ mammals

## Groups

| | | |
|---|---|---|
| 52. A group of objects related by definition. | a. | Ring |
| 53. A group of objects containing other groups of objects. | b. | Set |
| 54. A set of two or more sets including the union and differences of the sets. | c. | Subset |
| 55. A group of objects representing only parts a larger group. | d. | Superset |

a. Intersect
b. Element
c. Subset
d. Set
e. Union

# Unit 5—Programming & Coding

## Objectives:

Students will understand:

| | |
|---|---|
| 1. Terminology | 4. Programming Process |
| 2. Systems Development Life Cycle | 5. Data Structures |
| 3. Purpose of Systems Logic | 6. Control Structures |

## Terminology

| Term | Definition |
|---|---|
| Applet | Java scripts used in web documents that run in the browser window. |
| Application Software | Programs stored permanently on the computer and used to tell the computer how to produce information. |
| ASCII | American Standard Code for Information Interchange: the most widely used data coding system primarily for mini-computers and PCs. |
| Assembly Language | The first symbolic programming language. Is hardware specific but much easier to write than Machine Language. Must be converted into machine language in order to work though, using an Assembler. |
| Backtracking | The systematic way of exploring every possible route, configuration or ordering of an arrangement without repeating a path that was already explored. |
| BASIC | Beginner's All-Purpose Symbolic Instruction Code: Developed in the 60s to be a simple, interactive, problem-solving language that uses elementary English words combined with some symbology. Requires an interpreter to work (either built into the system ROM as with old PCs or in a program). |
| C | Programming language designed to create system software, including applications and operating systems. Most frequently used with UNIX. |
| C++ | Object Oriented version of C used to develop applications. |
| Class | A large category of objects, wherein the category helps define a characteristic shared by all the members (objects) of the group (class). |
| COBOL | Common Business Oriented Language: Widely used programming language for business that uses English-like commands. |
| Code Standards | Set by the American National Standards Institute to ensure programs are compatible with many different computers. |
| Coding | The process of translating and entering a process into a programming language (code) on a computer. |
| Compiler | The program that converts the code of a program into Machine Language. |
| Context Diagram | Top-level diagram of data flow that only shows major components of a process. |
| Control Structure | The instructions that control the order in which program instructions are executed. |
| Cooperative Multitasking | Method of managing multiple processes to insure they receive the information they need when they need it, and deliver their output when it is needed by other processes by switching between processes until logical stopping points are reach. |
| Data | The raw facts, including numbers, words, images, and sounds given as input to be processed. Data may be entered manually, embedded in the program, or from other sources. |
| Decoding | Translates instructions into processable commands. |
| Divide and Conquer | Process of breaking a large problem into smaller problems, solving the smaller problems then recombining the results to yield a solution to the large problem. |

| Entity | An object for which data is stored to define it. |
|---|---|
| Event | The pressing of a key, clicking of the mouse button, or other input impulse that provides data prompting action or providing data for action in an Object Oriented Program. |
| Executing | Control unit operation that processes commands. |
| Flowchart | A graphic representation of the logical flow of information through specific processes resulting in the desired output. |
| Fourth-Generation Language | A non-procedural language using English-like statements, that does not require being told how to perform an action, only what actions to perform. These programs are run within other programs, such as HTML, and Macros. |
| Graphic User Interface | (GUI) User interface using visual clues to aid in inputting data. |
| Greedy Heuristic | A method which attempts to capture the first possible greatest thing. |
| Heuristic | A trial and error approach to problem resolution that may give a kind of solution with no guarantee of success or accuracy. |
| Hierarchy | A logical ordering of information into classes and lesser subclasses inheriting the qualities of the higher ranking classes directly above the item. |
| Hierarchy Chart | A top-down design tool graphically representing program modules. |
| If-then-else Control Structure | Structure that evaluates conditions to determine if they are or are not true, and to take action accordingly. |
| Infinite Loop | Instructions that repeat themselves indefinitely. |
| Information | Data processed into meaningful and useful form. |
| Information Processing Cycle | The operations of input, process, output, storage. |
| Inheritance | The condition in which objects, including subclasses, keep the methods and attributes of objects and classes at higher levels of the program's hierarchy. |
| Interpreter | A process of converting command lines one at a time into machine language and executing them. |
| Java | Object-Oriented language very similar to C++, but more compact and offering greater user security. |
| JavaScript | Simpler form of Java that is not compiled and runs directly in a web browser. |
| Language Translator | A program that converts programming instructions one at a time into binary code and immediately executes them. |
| Machine Language | The binary codes which a computer or device acts upon. This is a hardware-specific language. |
| Module | Section of a program dedicated to performing a single function. |
| Object | Any piece of information created with a Windows program, which is linked or embedded in another application. In OOP a unit in which both data and procedure are packaged together. Objects are like elevators: you get on as data, push a button and are fed out as information on the desired floor. The elevator contains the information necessary to regulate its own processes initiated by you, the event. |
| Object Code | The machine language result of compiling a third-generation program. |
| Object-Oriented | Approach in which data and process are packaged together. |
| Object-Oriented Programming (OOP) Language | The event-driven programming language used to implement the object model design. |
| Operand | Specifies the data or location of the data to be used. |

| Output | Data processed in a form useful to the user or the computer (see also information). |
|---|---|
| Process | The transformation and output of data into a meaningful and useful form. |
| Program | Detailed set of instructions telling the computer exactly where to get data and how to process it. |
| RAM Computation Model | Model used for estimating the processing time of an algorithm. Each individual access of memory, and simple operation (e.g. +, -, *, =, if, call) takes one step. Loop structures must be computed by adding each individual element, as stated above. This model is not exact due to differences in machines, but does give a rough estimate. |
| Rapid Application Development | (RAD) A means of developing programs using prototypes (e.g. templates) that are easily modified to meet the program's needs. |
| Selection Control Structure | Tells the computer the action to take under the specified (e.g. event) condition. |
| Sequence | The order in which actions occur. |
| Sequence Control Structure | Shows one action or an action followed by another sequential action. |
| Solution Algorithm | Graphic or written step-by-step description of procedures within a module. |
| Source | Where information or an object originates from. Also the uncompiled code of a program. |
| Structured Design | Method of creating the program's logic using a combination of the sequence, selection, and repetition control structures. |
| Subclass | A class within a class, e.g. a subset. |
| Superclass | A class in which the current class belongs as a subset. |
| Symbolic Address | Storage location noted by a symbolic name in Assembly Language. |
| Symbolic Instruction Codes | (Mnemonics) Meaningful abbreviations for instructions used in Assembly Language. |
| Symbolic Language | Instructions are written using codes and symbols rather than zeros and ones. |
| Syntax | The set of grammatical rules of a programming language applied to instructions in a program. |
| Syntax Error | Any programming syntax mistake made in coding which results in the inability to complete the command. |
| System Flowchart | Graphic representation illustrating a major process, its timing, the output, data sources required, and necessary input devices. |
| Third-Generation Language | (Procedural Language) A high-level programming language using English-like words and mathematical notations to create processes. These must be compiled into Machine Language and often rely on environmental (e.g. operating system) components to perform many tasks. |
| Unstructured Problems | Problems with unclear methods leading toward their solutions, often requiring intuition and personal judgment (e.g. guessing and educated guessing). |
| Variable | An element of data in an object-oriented program. Technically any data element subject to variation depending on the source of the data (as opposed to internal constants). Variables are subject to change, and hence the root of the word: vary. |

## System Development Life Cycle

The flowchart to the right illustrates the Systems Development Life Cycle (SDLC). This cycle is remarkably comprehensive. It easily fits into any project development (business, education, law, any area of research), not to mention its applications with computer hardware, software and applications.

We observe that the cycle begins where it ends. This is not typical for flowcharts, but in this case the flow is a perfect cycle. The SDLC is continuous because needs are always changing as is the technology. Let us quickly examine each of these stages.

### Begin SDLC

Everything has a beginning. In the case of the SDLC the beginning of one cycle coincides with the ending of another (or others combined).

### Preliminary Investigation

What exists? At this stage you are merely asking what you have to work with (hardware, software, human resources, and any other necessary resource) and what it actually produces.

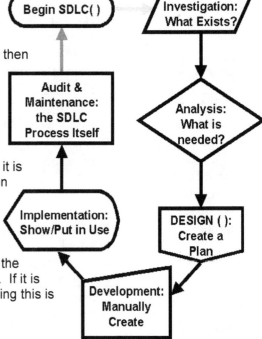

### Analysis

What is needed? If something is lacking or can be improved upon, then it is needed. The next part of this question is in what form must it be in? To answer this you must also know how the results will be applied to other things (e.g. in the preliminary investigation.

### Design

Create a plan. How will you fill the need? Can you buy something already developed cheaper, more easily and in the time it is needed, or must you personally create it? If you must create it, then how? This is the stage where flowcharting occurs to help visually define the plan, its sequence and methods.

### Development

Manually create/execute the plan. If it is a purchase, then execute the necessary process to make the purchase, install, train and utilize it. If it is something you must create from scratch, then do so. In programming this is the point when the plan is coded (put into a programing language).

### Implementation

Show/put to use the completed plan. All innovation and technology are on-going tests. It seems we test them, debug them, and test them again at this stage, but really we are going through the whole SDLC process. Implementation includes testing in the lab and actual application by "end-users."

### Audit & Maintenance

The SDLC process itself is a process of auditing processes, updating and maintaining them to meet current needs. In information technology the process runs very quickly because there are so many demands and so many individuals and copanies racing to meet those demands.

## Purpose of Systems Logic

The fundamental logic of computer operations is systematic: step-by-step procedures. A text may tell you what to do to manipulate a file a certain way. A reference may break down each function of a program and even give examples. Neither the text nor the reference tell you how to manipulate every file. Each file poses an unique problem requiring the computer operator to determine a procedure for filling the file requirements. This text attempts to combine all three of these by providing step-by-step procedures in a reference format, followed by activities that utilize those procedures. To use this text effectively, you must be able to understand the elementary logic of computing. The elementary logic of computing is the System Development Life Cycle (SDLC) in which components are described using flowcharts.

## Programming Process

| | |
|---|---|
| 1. Identify Program Function | 4. Identify Specific Processes and Data |
| 2. Identify the Platform | 5. Create Flowcharts for Objects |
| 3. Identify Non-Programming Alternatives | 6. Create Objects and Test |

***Identify Program Function***

What do you need the program to do?

❑ Common functions: graphics, word processing, file management, calculating, etc. These are almost always removed (running in something else).

❑ Technical functions: utilities, operating system, hardware configuration, etc. If the program is not removed, then it directly communicates with the computer system in machine language. That means the binary code must be compatible with the hardware involved.

❑ Removed functions: must be run within another program (e.g. within Windows or other operating system, a Browser, etc.). Most programs are in some way removed (e.g. are running in another program). The question here is really: "Removed to what?"

❑ Special functions: works within a unique environment (not a typical

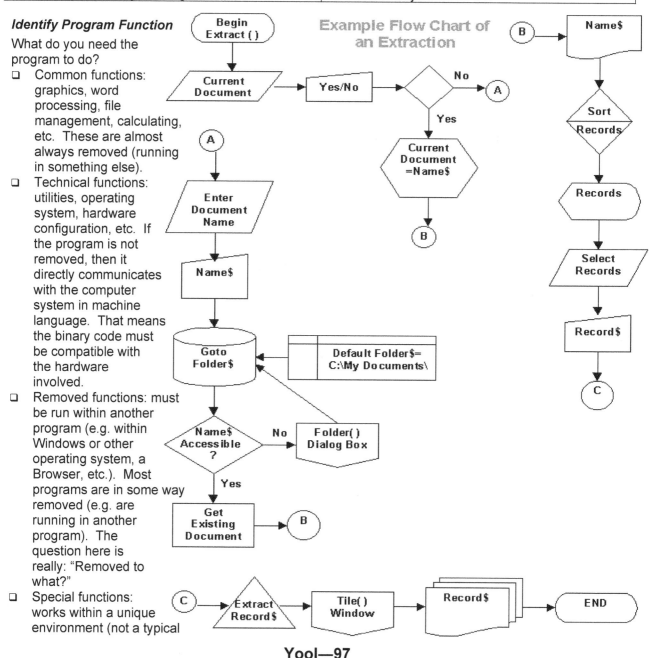

computer environment, like automobiles, cellular phones, calculators, robots).  These are typically in machine language and designed specifically to meet the needs of input and output components as well as any computational and memory features (if any).

### Identify the Platform

What will be running/executing the program?  The program is removed by what?
a.  Nothing: directly addresses computer components in machine language without requiring other programs.  What are the code requirements for the hardware?
b.  Requires an Operating System: relies on features filled in by the operating system to perform its functions.  These are Third Generation Programs.  Note: BASIC was and remains Third Generation.  Old computers used to keep their operating systems in ROM (Read-Only Memory) along with translating features to convert the code into actions.  Question is: In what operating system/platform.
c.  Requires a Program within an Operating System: relies on features of a third generation program to Translate/Interpret its functions.  These are Fourth and Fifth (Natural) Generation Languages.  These include SQL and other query languages, macros, and Hypertext Markup Language (HTML).  Question is: In what Third Generation program?

### Identify Non-Programming Alternatives

a.  Does a non-programming alternative exist that is more practical?
b.  Is there a non-computer method that can provide the necessary results?
c.  Would the non-computer method be more practical (e.g. time wise, financially, labor and other resources wise)?
d.  Can one or more programs provide the necessary results?
e.  Can they be integrated for a complete end product as needed?
f.  How can they be integrated?

### Identify Specific Processes and Data

a.  Divide the program into distinct functions that may be sequenced separately.
b.  Divide each function into data and actions necessary to perform the function.
c.  Simplify data into the least number of necessary variables.  If a variable may change from one action to another, create a separate variable for each.  If each of these unique variables has an identical default, then create a simple default statement in the appropriate class.
d.  Associate actions with the data variables and determine which variables are shared, universal, or "private" to that action.
e.  Put universal values in a class within the hierarchy above the actions that call on them and label them as shared.
f.  Put shared variables with their specific actions (sequences) and label them as shared.
g.  Put the private variables with their specific actions (sequences) and label them as private.

### Create Objects and Test

a.  Routine Flowcharts: The flowchart provides a logical sequence of events including gathering, manipulating and outputting information.  Each function must have a logical sequence to provide step-by-step exact actions needed to complete the function.  Be sure to think of every possible thing that could cause a process to fail (e.g. bad or missing data) and to provide alternative means of inputting the data manually before the process tries to use it.
b.  Create Primary Object: The primary object is also called the Source.  It must contain means of contacting, either directly or indirectly, all the function sequences.  It is itself a sequence and the primary interface between the computer, software, data and user.
c.  Identify Appropriate Language: The language must fit the environment the program will run in and the function needs of the program.  Not all environments support the same functions.  As such sometimes it

is necessary to change the environment to meet the needs of the programming language needed to execute the functions.

d. Translate into Appropriate Language: Convert the sequences you have written into the codes necessary to do them.

e. Organize and Compile as Needed: Put all the objects of the program in a logical sequence with distinct boundaries (e.g. separate files, grouped by class distinction, line numbered, etc. as appropriate to the language and application). Compiling translates the programming language you used to write the program into Machine Language.

f. Test and Debug: Every program, regardless of its simplicity or language, has potential for failure. Failures may be syntax, incorrect sequencing, mislabeled connections or data, etc. Errors are remarkably easy to make and immeasurably difficult at times to find in the code (certainly easy when executing the program to see the error in the output though!). To debug you must find the error in the program and correct it. Then test again to be sure the problem has not persisted and that other problems did not surface.

## Data Structures

### Data Types

| | |
|---|---|
| Constant | A value applied to a name within the code of a program. For example you might define Pi=3.14159265358979 so you do not need to retype the number repeatedly, and to conserve the size of your program. |
| String | Textual data type. See also String under Data Storage & Retrieval. |
| Variable | A name applied to a number whose source is either user input or the result of a formula. These often have initial values. They are called variables because the value is subject to change. |
| Public | Denotes a value (textual or quantitative) may be used by any subclass within a class. A common use for this is with constants which may be used by any routine with a superclass, or any variable which must be accessed by another class. |
| Private | Denotes a value (textual or quantitative) may be used only within the class where it resides. Commonly use counting functions, because the counter typically resides within the local function only. |

### Variable Containers

| Type | Value Range | Purpose | Memory Size |
|---|---|---|---|
| Char | Plain text | Plain text | 8 bits |
| Short int | ±255 | Small integers (whole numbers) | 8 bits |
| Int | -32,768 to 32,767 | Integers (whole numbers) | 16 bits |
| Long Integer | -2,147,483,648 to 2,147,483,647 | Large integers (whole numbers) | 32 bits |
| Float | ±3.402823E38 to ±1.401298E-45 | Real numbers (with decimal values) | 32 bits |
| Double | ±1.79769313486232E308 to ±4.94065645841247E-324 | Extremely large real numbers. | 64 bits |

### Data Storage

| | |
|---|---|
| Array | A collection of data items with a single name distinguished by numbers. In BASIC you can define an array with five elements by using DIM X(5), then later define the values for those elements {X(1), X(2), X(3), X(4), X(5)} separately. An array may be multidimensional such that information is accessed as if in a table by row and column numbers (e.g. DIM Y(5,5) allows 25 elements). |
| Graph | Geometric representation of the relationships between two or more objects (illustrates coordinates, distance and angle). Most likely of issue when dealing with a network, circuit, |

| | |
|---|---|
| | web, or relationship. |
| List | A set of data items to be accessed in order. |
| Permutation | An arrangement or ordering of items, e.g. {1, 2, 3, 4} and {4, 3, 2, 1} are two permutations of the same set.  Often synonymous with arrangement, tour, ordering, and sequence. |
| String | A sequence of characters or patterns.  Strings are typically of issue when dealing with text, characters, patterns, or labels. |
| Tree | A hierarchical representation of relationships between items.  An example would be the hierarchy of folders on your computer, or a family tree.  Trees are typically of issue when dealing with a hierarchy, dominance relationship, ancestor/descendent relationship, or taxonomy. |

### Data Retrieval

| | |
|---|---|
| Container | A data retrieval structure independent of the actual data.  These are typically used with data sets and not with variables with only a single value. |
| Queue | The retrieval of information according to First-In-First-Out (FIFO) priority.  Queues may be prioritized according to significance, or placed in a specific sequence if the objects must be attained in a specific order.  Print jobs are typically set to queue in the order they are created in.  Typically when printing from a laser printer you want the pages to come out first to last so they appear (queue) in order. |
| Stack | The retrieval of information according to Last-In-First-Out priority.  When retrieval order does not matter, (e.g. batch processing) then a stack may be appropriate.  When printing to a DeskJet or other printer that feeds the output face-up, you want the job stacked so the last page prints first, and the first page prints last. |
| Table | Retrieves information according to position.  This is the method you use when retrieving information from an array. |

## Control Structures

### Switch

A function that swaps one value or set for another.  Microsoft Excel has a set of functions called lookups (lookup, hlookup, and vlookup).  As an example of a switch examine the following method for the MOUS exam and example of vlookup.

### Method:
1. If the range name is given in the question, start at step 4.
2. Click the second sheet tab
3. Click the down arrow on the name box and select the named range (remember the name!)
4. Click the first sheet tab
5. Select the cell where you will enter the function in column B
6. Type: **=vlookup(**
7. Type the name of the range you looked up in step 2 then type: ,
8. Select the range of cells being used for the lookup (both columns and all rows) then type: ,**2)**
9. Click and drag the fill handle down through the desired cells.

**Example:**

| Sheet1 | | |
|---|---|---|
| | **A** | **B** |
| **2** | Label | Return Value |
| **3** | D | Banana |
| **4** | C | Grape |
| **5** | A | Orange |
| **6** | B | Apple |
| **7** | | |
| **8** | | |

### Function in Column B of Sheet1

=vlookup(a3,RangeName,2)
=vlookup(a4,RangeName,2)
=vlookup(a5,RangeName,2)
=vlookup(a6,RangeName,2)
Note: The highlighted cells on the right are named RangeName.

| Sheet2 | | |
|---|---|---|
| | **A** | **B** |
| **2** | | |
| **3** | | |
| **4** | Label | Description |
| **5** | A | Orange |
| **6** | B | Apple |
| **7** | C | Grape |
| **8** | D | Banana |

### Loops

Loops serve a variety of functions including counting, making decisions, and any function that requires repetition of the same sequence (typically in association with a counting function). Loops can easily become indefinite with the result of system lock-up and program failure, so it is highly advised to provide means of escaping your loops before system or data resources are exhausted. The loops we will examine here include the post-test Do-While, the pre-test While, the decisive If-Else, the swapping Switch, and counting For statements. I associate the terms decisive, swapping and counting to the latter functions because that is most descriptive of their common functions. Swapping may also be done in a more cumbersome way with the If-Else, decisions will to occur in all these types of loops, and counting commonly occurs in all but the Switch.

## Switch Statement

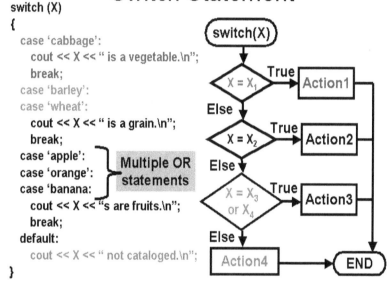

```
switch (X)
{
    case 'cabbage':
        cout << X << " is a vegetable.\n";
        break;
    case 'barley':
    case 'wheat':
        cout << X << " is a grain.\n";
        break;
    case 'apple':
    case 'orange':
    case 'banana:
        cout << X << "s are fruits.\n";
        break;
    default:
        cout << X << " not cataloged.\n";
}
```

Multiple OR statements

## Do-While Statement

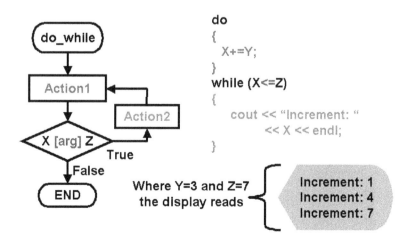

```
do
{
    X+=Y;
}
while (X<=Z)
{
    cout << "Increment: "
        << X << endl;
}
```

Where Y=3 and Z=7 the display reads

Increment: 1
Increment: 4
Increment: 7

# If-Else Loop

```
if (X<Y)
{
    cout << X << " < " << Y << endl;
}
else
{
    if (X=Y)
        cout << X << " = " << Y << endl;
    else
        cout << Y << " < " << X << endl;
}
```

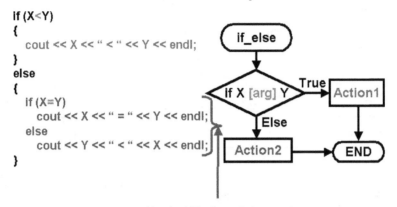

Nested if-else statement

# For Loop

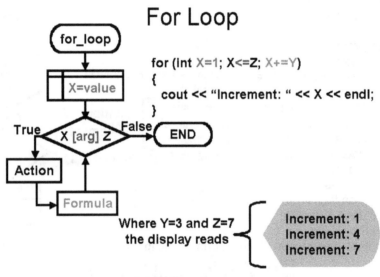

```
for (int X=1; X<=Z; X+=Y)
{
    cout << "Increment: " << X << endl;
}
```

Where Y=3 and Z=7
the display reads

Increment: 1
Increment: 4
Increment: 7

# While Loop

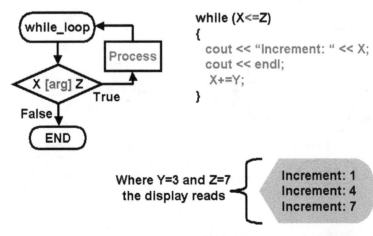

```
while (X<=Z)
{
    cout << "Increment: " << X;
    cout << endl;
    X+=Y;
}
```

Where Y=3 and Z=7
the display reads

Increment: 1
Increment: 4
Increment: 7

**Yool—102**

## Nested Function

A function within a like function. For example, $f(X)=f(Y) + f(Z)$. Word 2000 supports nested tables. This means you can insert a table into a table cell. The most common function to nest is the If-Else (see table):

| Lengthy: | Short: |
|---|---|
| If X=1<br>{<br>    Y=A;<br>}<br>Else if X=2<br>{<br>    Y=B;<br>}<br>Else<br>{<br>    Y=C;<br>} | If X=1<br>{<br>    Y=A;<br>}<br>if X=2<br>{<br>    Y=B;<br>}<br>Y=C; |

## Recursion

Any process that references itself to perform its function. For example, X=X+1 is recursive.

# Recursion

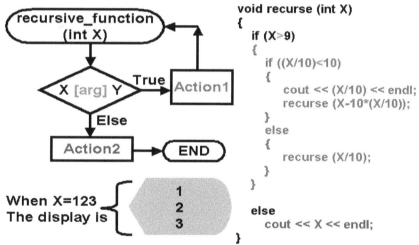

```
void recurse (int X)
{
    if (X>9)
    {
        if ((X/10)<10)
        {
            cout << (X/10) << endl;
            recurse (X-10*(X/10));
        }
        else
        {
            recurse (X/10);
        }
    }
    else
        cout << X << endl;
}
```

When X=123
The display is
1
2
3

# Worksheet 5—Programming & Coding

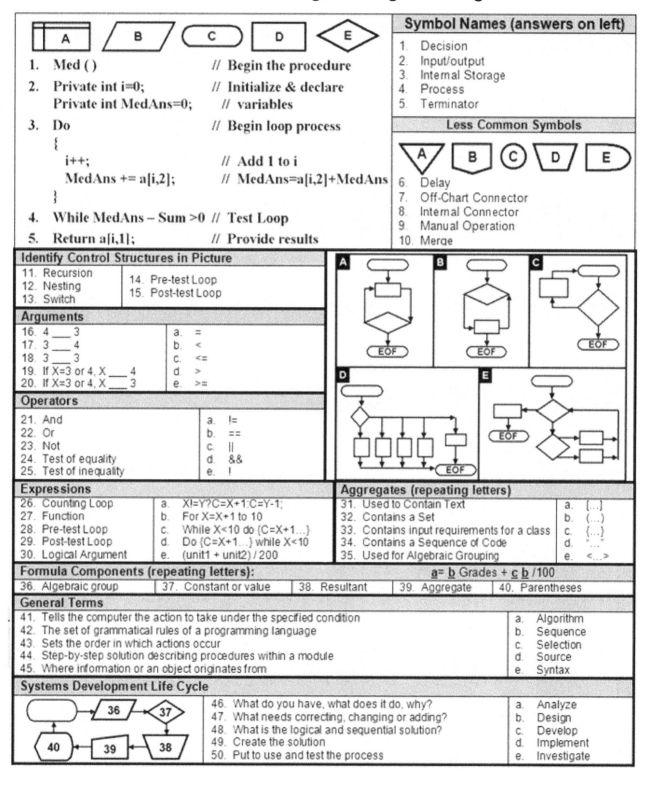

| | | | | |
|---|---|---|---|---|
| A | B | C | D | E |

1. Med ( )                    // **Begin the procedure**
2. Private int i=0;           // **Initialize & declare**
   Private int MedAns=0;      // **variables**
3. Do                         // **Begin loop process**
   {
     i++;                     // **Add 1 to i**
     MedAns += a[i,2];        // **MedAns=a[i,2]+MedAns**
   }
4. While MedAns – Sum >0      // **Test Loop**
5. Return a[i,1];             // **Provide results**

### Symbol Names (answers on left)

1. Decision
2. Input/output
3. Internal Storage
4. Process
5. Terminator

### Less Common Symbols

| A | B | C | D | E |
|---|---|---|---|---|

6. Delay
7. Off-Chart Connector
8. Internal Connector
9. Manual Operation
10. Merge

### Identify Control Structures in Picture

11. Recursion
12. Nesting
13. Switch

14. Pre-test Loop
15. Post-test Loop

### Arguments

| 16. 4 ___ 3 | a. = |
|---|---|
| 17. 3 ___ 4 | b. < |
| 18. 3 ___ 3 | c. <= |
| 19. If X=3 or 4, X ___ 4 | d. > |
| 20. If X=3 or 4, X ___ 3 | e. >= |

### Operators

| 21. And | a. != |
|---|---|
| 22. Or | b. == |
| 23. Not | c. \|\| |
| 24. Test of equality | d. && |
| 25. Test of inequality | e. ! |

### Expressions

| 26. Counting Loop | a. X!=Y?C=X+1:C=Y-1; |
|---|---|
| 27. Function | b. For X=X+1 to 10 |
| 28. Pre-test Loop | c. While X<10 do {C=X+1...} |
| 29. Post-test Loop | d. Do {C=X+1...} while X<10 |
| 30. Logical Argument | e. (unit1 + unit2) / 200 |

### Aggregates (repeating letters)

| 31. Used to Contain Text | a. [...] |
|---|---|
| 32. Contains a Set | b. (...) |
| 33. Contains input requirements for a class | c. {...} |
| 34. Contains a Sequence of Code | d. "..." |
| 35. Used for Algebraic Grouping | e. <...> |

### Formula Components (repeating letters):     $\underline{a}$= $\underline{b}$ Grades + $\underline{c}$ $\underline{b}$ /100

| 36. Algebraic group | 37. Constant or value | 38. Resultant | 39. Aggregate | 40. Parentheses |
|---|---|---|---|---|

### General Terms

| 41. Tells the computer the action to take under the specified condition | a. Algorithm |
|---|---|
| 42. The set of grammatical rules of a programming language | b. Sequence |
| 43. Sets the order in which actions occur | c. Selection |
| 44. Step-by-step solution describing procedures within a module | d. Source |
| 45. Where information or an object originates from | e. Syntax |

### Systems Development Life Cycle

| | 46. What do you have, what does it do, why? | a. Analyze |
|---|---|---|
| | 47. What needs correcting, changing or adding? | b. Design |
| | 48. What is the logical and sequential solution? | c. Develop |
| | 49. Create the solution | d. Implement |
| | 50. Put to use and test the process | e. Investigate |

## Data Structures

| | |
|---|---|
| 51. A series of values attributed to a name. | a. Array |
| 52. A hierarchical representation of relationships between items. | b. List |
| 53. An arrangement or ordering of items. | c. String |
| 54. A matrix of values attributed to a name. | d. Permutation |
| 55. A sequence of characters or patterns. | e. Tree |

## Data Types

| | |
|---|---|
| 56. Denotes value of the data name may be used by any class. | a. Public |
| 57. A value applied to a name within the code of a program. | b. Private |
| 58. Textual data type or a sequence of characters or patterns. | c. Constant |
| 59. Denotes value of the data name may be used only within the class where it resides. | d. Variable |
| 60. A name applied to a number whose source is either user input or a formula result. | e. Text |

## Data Retrieval (repeating letters)

| | |
|---|---|
| 61. The retrieval of information according to Last-In-First-Out priority. | a. Table |
| 62. The retrieval of information according to First-In-First-Out (FIFO) priority. | b. Queue |
| 63. Retrieves information according to position. | c. Container |
| 64. A data retrieval structure independent of the actual data. | d. Stack |
| 65. This is the method you use when retrieving information from an array. | |

## Languages

| | | |
|---|---|---|
| 66. Says what to do but not how | 71. Hardware specific in binary | a. Assembly Language |
| 67. C++ and Java are examples | 72. Created and used in the same program | b. Fifth Generation |
| 68. Hardware and symbolic | 73. One routine does a class of actions | c. Fourth Generation |
| 69. Requires an interpreter | 74. Compiling transfers symbols to this | d. Machine Language |
| 70. SQL is an example | 75. Must be compiled to run | e. Third Generation |

## Completing a Program

| | |
|---|---|
| 76. Converting an entire hardware specific symbolic program into computable commands | a. Interpreting |
| 77. Converting an entire non-hardware specific symbolic program into computable commands | b. Decoding |
| 78. Converting one command line at a time and executing it | c. Compiling |
| 79. Translating and inputting a process into a programming language on the computer | d. Coding |
| 80. Translating instructions into process-able commands | e. Assembling |

## Third Generation Superstructure

| | |
|---|---|
| 81. Something for which data is stored to define it (e.g. the pot in the flowchart above) | a. Class |
| 82. Section of a program dedicated to performing a specific action | b. Entity |
| 83. Logical ordering into groups and subgroups inheriting qualities of higher ranking groups | c. Hierarchy |
| 84. Large category defining a characteristic shared by its members | d. Module |
| 85. A Unit in which both data and procedure are packaged together | e. Object |

## Logical Structures

| | |
|---|---|
| 86. A logical process defining sequence, selection, and repetition | a. Control Structure |
| 87. Method of combining sequence, selection, and repetition to create a program's logic | b. Flow Chart |
| 88. Method of graphically illustrating the logic of a process | c. Object Oriented |
| 89. Event-driven, encapsulates data and process, supporting inheritance and polymorphism | d. Program |
| 90. Set of detailed instructions stating exactly where to get data and how to process it | e. Structured Design |

## Controlling Things

| | |
|---|---|
| 91. Using the definition of an object to define one or more of its own components (x=x+1) | a. Event |
| 92. Retaining and using methods and attributes from superior groups of procedures | b. Fetch |
| 93. Process whereby the computer (CPU) acquires the next set of command instructions | c. Inheritance |
| 94. Pressing a key, clicking or any other action providing information the computer acts on | d. Loop |
| 95. Any process in which a component returns to and repeats earlier instructions | e. Recursion |

## Coding Qualities

| | |
|---|---|
| 96. Superclass of a program providing access to all other classes. | a. Polymorphism |
| 97. Quality allowing a program to isolate variables within or share data among classes. | b. Encapsulation |
| 98. Using the same name for two different functions, differentiable by the number or types of arguments. | c. Main Class |
| 99. Quality allowing one routine to do a class of actions. | d. Pointer |
| 100. A variable containing an address to another location in the code. | e. Overload |

# Unit 6—Problem Solving

## Objectives:
Students will understand:

| | |
|---|---|
| 1. RAM Model<br>2. Problem Solving With Reasoning | 3. Graph Problems |

## RAM Model
The Random Access Machine (RAM) Model is used to determine the processing speed of an algorithm. To assist understanding how this model works we will examine a RAM model applied to web pages then examine the same concept applied to algorithms and programming.

### Web Design RAM Model

Fundamental Principles:

- All computations are relative
- Assume browser processing is >= connection
- 3 units = server script execution or absolute reference

- 1 unit =
  - 1000 bytes of information
  - Relative call for data
  - Invocation of styles or scripts
  - Style execution, module call, class execution
  - ASP results processing

The following table outlines the relative time it takes to acquire and view information for a web page in a browser. The reader could use the same table layout to make design decisions for any site. Notice that all objects are given integer values regardless of size due to the fact that each piece is individually packaged during transmission. Below the table is a brief description of each attribute.

| | | Size | Calls | Function | QTY | Time |
|---|---|---|---|---|---|---|
| No Frames | HTML (typical page entry with navigation) | 2 | 1 | 0 | | |
| | Background Image | 1 | 1 | 0 | | |
| | Significant images | 1 | 1 | 0 | | |
| | Singular toolbar | 2 | 1 | 0 | | |
| | Embedded Styles | 1 | 0 | 1 | | |
| | Linked Styles | 1 | 1 | 1 | | |
| | Scripts | 1 | 0 | 1 | | |
| | Buttons as Separate Images | 1 | 1 | 0 | | |
| Frames | HTML (typical page entry with navigation) | 1 | 1 | 0 | 3 | |
| | Background Image | 1 | 1 | 0 | | |
| | Significant images | 1 | 1 | 0 | | |
| | Singular toolbar | 2 | 1 | 0 | | |
| | Embedded Styles | 1 | 0 | 1 | | |
| | Linked Styles | 1 | 1 | 1 | | |
| | Scripts | 1 | 0 | 1 | | |
| | Buttons as Separate Images | 1 | 1 | 0 | | |

Size—For HTML and other documents, this is determined by the file size rounded up to the nearest kilobyte (1024 bits of information). For scripts the number of classes, not the number of commands, determines size. For particularly long classes, say over 20 command lines, I would recommend adjusting this value following the standard RAM model applied to programs, as the browser must interpret each individual line of code.

Worksheet 5—Programming & Coding

Unit 6—Problem Solving

Calls—Referencing an object on the server. If you are referencing a CGI script, then add 3. This chart assumes relative references (valued at 1 unit), where absolute references (citing the entire URL) should be counted as 3 instead.

Function—Functions are only applied to Styles and Scripts because these are not the primary native format of a browser, so the browser needs to invoke other subroutines to interpret the code. Each time the code is invoked requires the addition of 1 unit, no matter how many lines of code are involved.

QTY—How many instances of the Web object occur. For Styles, every individual style is counted as a unit because the browser must interpret then apply the individual item throughout the document. For Scripts, each class is treated separately as a unit.

Time—The sum of Size, Calls, Function multiplied by the quantity. The sum total of these times gives you an idea of how long it takes to load the page.

I seriously discourage the use of both styles and scripts. Styles are not supported the same among browsers. If you use them, I recommend keeping them very simple because Internet Explorer and Netscape produce very different results. Personally I recommend using HTML instead. VB script and ActiveX are only recognized by Internet Explorer. All browsers encounter problems interpreting Java Script, resulting in browser failure during page loading or other attempts to access the code.

A major error of web designers is the use of multiple graphic objects when one will suffice, such as with buttons. I encourage integrating your images and using image-mapping techniques with HTML. Always create the image the size you want it to be on the page then you do not need to worry about defining the size in the HTML, nor do you need to worry about the resolution of the image nor file size. Although I recommend embedding special fonts in graphics, I would also encourage you to refrain from too large of graphics and encourage you to provide enough text to occupy the viewer until graphics appear.

### RAM in Algorithms

Fundamental principles of RAM cycles in algorithms:

- All basic functions = 1 unit/ cycle (+, -, *, =, memory access)
- Loops are composites of their parts
- Division is a function of the solving algorithm

RAM applied to algorithms provides nothing more than a concision meter. In other words, by counting the number of cycles required to process information at the algorithm stage you can compare algorithms for time efficiency. The key, of figure illustrates a basic sort 17 cycles, and the worst is 3 in worst). Some redundancy sort. A random selection of per item). A brute force sort the same set! While this sor efficient for larger sort jobs. and in the quicker method re small set, the sort time of the the case of a median, this qu and in fact it helps resolve in

### RAM in Programming

Back to Napoleon's: "The be your algorithm you become : can also save large amounts from observation the speed 5, and with 9 items yields 15 based on the number of item

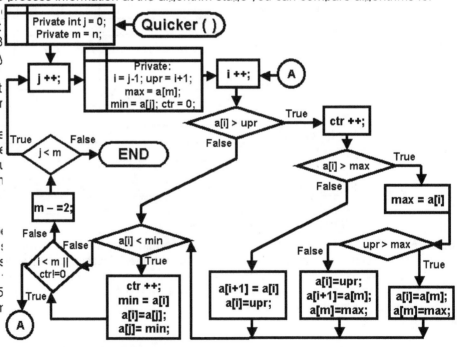

log n or even faster) or slower.  Note: The compiler will estimate the run-time for you.  The brute force sort can easily become n² with poor technique, e.g. variable miss-management.

## Problem Solving With Reasoning

There are two forms of reasoning: inductive (speculative) and deductive (analytical).  Inductive reasoning goes from the part to the whole, from the abstract to the concrete, from a few observations to a formula defining the whole.  Deductive reasoning goes from the whole to the part, from the concrete to the abstract, deriving the specific from a formula.

### *Elements of Inductive Reasoning*

### Define (Facilitative)
- What does this topic mean (the definition)?
- What are the parts of this definition?

F1. Composite initiate—What is the general, accepted definition?
F2. Constructive bonds—What fundamental concepts (components: action, subject, object) are brought together by the definition?
F3. Correlate bond-action—What are the relationships between the components of the definition?
F4. Relative action—How do these correlations affect the definition?
F5. Initiate action—What do these affects infer about similar systems?

### Operate (Formulative)
- What process does the topic represent?
    - O1.    What is the real form of this stimulus?
    - O2.    What concept do we perceive of this stimulus?
    - O3.    How do we present or represent the concept?
    - O4.    How do we relate the concept to other stimuli?

### Method (Fundamental)
- What can be measured in the defined system?

A1. Affective—What is the action?
A2. Effective—What is the subject?
A3. Effectual—What is the object (result)?

### Philosophical Inference (Functional)
- How do we measure the component parts of the definition?

P1. Thesis—What must exist for the process to occur?
P2. Antithesis—What must exist for the opposite of the process to occur?

### Holistic Axiom (Foundational)
- This is the absolute, transcendental real, that which is perceived, the impulse, but not to be mistaken for the perception thereof.
- What general principle (axiom) always exists given these values?
    H1. Synthesis—What exists?

### *Elements of Deductive Reasoning*

### Holistic Axiom (Foundational)
- This is the absolute, transcendental real, that which is perceived, the impulse, but not to be mistaken for the perception thereof.
- What general principle (axiom) always exists given these values?
    - H1.    Synthesis—What exists?

### Philosophical Inference (Functional)

Worksheet 5—Programming & Coding
Unit 6—Problem Solving
- How do we measure the component parts of the definition?
  P1. Thesis—What must exist for the process to occur?
  P2. Antithesis—What must exist for the opposite of the process to occur?

## Method (Fundamental)
- What can be measured in the defined system?
  A1. Affective—What is the action?
  A2. Effective—What is the subject?
  A3. Effectual—What is the object (result)?

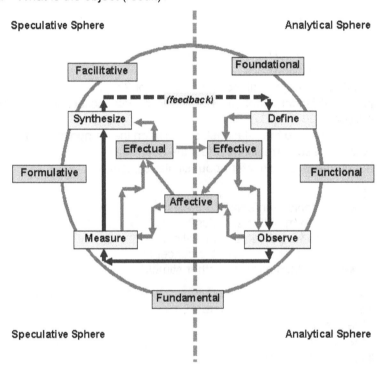

## Operate (Formulative)
- What process does the topic represent?
  O1.    What is the real form of this stimulus?
  O2.    What concept do we perceive of this stimulus?
  O3.    How do we present or represent the concept?
  O4.    How do we relate the concept to other stimuli?

## Define (Facilitative)
- What does this topic mean (the definition)?
- What are the parts of this definition?
  F1.    Composite initiate—What is the general, accepted definition?
  F2.    Constructive bonds—What fundamental concepts (components: action, subject, object) are brought together by the definition?
  F3.    Correlate bond-action—What are the relationships between the components of the definition?
  F4.    Relative action—How do these correlations affect the definition?
  F5.    Initiate action—What do these affects infer about similar systems?

## Applying the Paradigm

The scientific method is a deductive (analytical) model. While it provides a lot of raw data and either proves or disproves solutions, it does not create solutions, e.g. algorithms. Algorithms are developed inductively, which is contrary to the normal thought process of most people, who are raised to follow formulas. As such, inductive thinking is a conscious act when most people do it. When we become conscious of a process of thinking it is equally easy to lose track of our normal thought process. To make matters worse, since most people are not thinking inductively, most have also not formalized their thinking. The few who have formalized deductive thinking either learned the formality or are natural inductive thinkers.

Neither system is infallible. It is dreadfully easy to find proof of virtually any theorem simply by picking the right set of values to test. Likewise it is dreadfully easy to create a theorem without examining a representative set of all possible values. As such, both must work together. To do this you may do a **split-half test**. The split-half test takes all known values and splits them into equal groups. For best results, make the selection randomly. Use the first group to develop the algorithm and the second to test the algorithm. Then, to further test your reliability, identify values that should fail the algorithm (the antithetical values, which are known with certainty to not belong to the set) and put them through also.

A common need in programming is program testers. Program testers purposefully check the limitations of programs and try to make them break. This is like turning your research paper over to an English professor for credit: better to have as few errors as possible. So the moral of the story is to be mindful of using both processes formally as they should be. When you have a lot of information and no formula for solution, start inductively to develop a formula. When you have, run test data to be sure it works in as many instances as possible, and imagine and test any data that could cause the process to fail. If the algorithm does not behave, then take that knowledge back to the inductive process and start over.

Now we have dealt with the fundamentals of solving the unsolved in general, let us examine how the Paradigm apples to information systems. The Paradigm of Paradigm Development may be applied to literally any field of knowledge. The Paradigm is a working model, meaning it may be applied to real problems and provides real results. The accuracy of these results is entirely dependent on the information fed into the Paradigm. To understand this information we should look at the five category sets: Metaphysical, Epistemological, Axiological, Paradological, Holistic.

The study of metaphysics is the study of that which is real, asking such questions as "What is the nature of reality?" For our purposes metaphysics asks questions regarding the interface and the nature of the data input and output. The stages of metaphysical examination as applied deductively to programming follow:

| Foundational | The primary concern at this stage is superficial, such as the interface versus function of the program. Here we examine the whole problem at once, Holistically.<br>• What do you want the program to do?<br>• What already exists that performs actions similar or equal to the desired actions?<br>• What qualities do similar products provide and how (e.g. interface)?<br>• How will yours be different, even better? |
|---|---|
| Functional | Here our concern is measuring things, such as how to measure accuracy, speed, and required resources. These measurements are always done as points along a spectrum of extremes: best to worst-case scenario. These are typically confused as belonging to Axiology, but actually belong to Paradology.<br>• What degree of accuracy is sought? How will we determine the degree of accuracy?<br>• How fast must the algorithm perform a task? How will we make this determination?<br>• How much system resources are available to perform the task?<br>• How soon must the solution be found? (Typically the faster a solution is needed the less accurate and fast it will be, and the more resources it will use) |
| Fundamental | Here we identify the actual measurable parts. This is the real objective of the field of Axiology in philosophy.<br>• Affective Values are those dealing with significance. For example, many algorithms may adequately suffice to calculate 100 digits of pi, but few can achieve 1000. Is it truly necessary? According to significance, no. Some individuals, however, do not |

| | |
|---|---|
| | know when enough is enough.<br>• Effective Values are those dealing with resources, such as how much is available and how.<br>• Effectual Values are those dealing with validity and reliability, establishing the degree of accuracy within the significant range. |
| Formulative | Here we identify the thinking parts, those parts requiring knowledge and the development thereof. This is the Epistemological realm of philosophy.<br>• Concrete: To what does our problem apply? You could even ask, "Who would be interested in using our program?<br>• Reflect: What is our program expected to do?<br>• Abstract: What do we know about the solution of our problem? e.g. What formulas exist?<br>• Concept: How do we apply the concepts of the existing formulas? |
| Facilitative | Finally we apply what we have learned and reverse the process to check ourselves. Of the metaphysical components, this belongs most to Metaphysics. Based on all other observations we can now consider our end product. This includes our interface, what our interface will do with input, what our program will do to manipulate, the relationship of manipulations to each other, and what our interface does with the output.<br>• What will our interface look like, and in what environment?<br>• How is information put into our interface? Are there menus, tools, buttons, a need for files and more permanent data retrieval and storage? Aside from telling the program what to do, how does the user provide raw data?<br>• How does this information appear? Is it formatted in some particular way?<br>• Does the interface perform manipulation before executing deeper manipulation commands?<br>• How does the program manipulate the information?<br>• What information does the interface receive from the deeper functions? How is this information displayed?<br>• Is the information stored for later use? If so how? Or is it sent to yet another application? |

## Graph Problems

| | |
|---|---|
| Acyclic | Having no directed cycles. |
| Adjacency Graph | An illustration showing the relationships between vertices. For example, a map or other graphical form which is most useful and easy for humans to interpret. |
| Adjacency List | Array of pointers used to show connectivity between vertices. Recommended for most applications. In the Adjacency Matrix above, A is connected to P and S so the list for A would look like A—P—S. |
| Adjacency Matrix | An n x n array of Boolean values showing connectivity between vertices. 0 indicates no connection while 1 indicates connection. Some authors prefer to use a 0 where vertices intersect themselves (A, A = 0). I am more optimistic and believe vertices should be their own "friends" and use a 1 to indicate a vertice is connected to itself. |

| | A | C | M | P | S | T |
|---|---|---|---|---|---|---|
| A | 1 | 0 | 0 | 1 | 1 | 0 |
| C | 0 | 1 | 1 | 1 | 1 | 1 |
| M | 0 | 1 | 1 | 1 | 1 | 0 |
| P | 1 | 1 | 1 | 1 | 1 | 0 |
| S | 1 | 1 | 1 | 1 | 1 | 0 |
| T | 0 | 1 | 0 | 0 | 0 | 1 |

| | |
|---|---|
| Articulation Vertex | A vertex that, if deleted, would disconnect the other vertices from each other. For example, friends who are exclusively your friends are indirectly connected to your family. Without you your family members may well never communicate with these friends unless they have edges joining them as friends too. |
| Binary Tree | Method of distributing ordered data that insures rapid access. The entire group is divided into two parts, wherein the right branch contains all values greater than the center value and the left branch contains all values lesser. Each branch is then similarly divided. |
| Clique | Group of vertices bound as a subset by joining edges. |
| Connected | Vertices share an edge. A Connected Component is a connected vertice in disconnected sets. |
| Degree | Number of edges intersecting (joining) a vertice. |
| Dense | Most vertices many joints. |
| Directed | Quality of an edge or group of edges indicating a one-way relationship (one-way road). |
| Edge | A line connecting two vertices (a vertex pair); denoted with an **E**. On a polyhedron the number of edges enclosing a single face is denoted with an **S**. |
| Face | An area outlined by edges; denoted with an **F**. Graphs illustrating the shortest route traveled among points without intersecting the same point twice do not have enclosed faces unless the traveler returns to the point of origin or a "hub" is used. |
| Forest | Undirected paths not connected at an end. |
| Girth | The shortest cycle of connected points. |
| Graph | An illustration of a group of related vertices or "points." |
| Hamiltonian Cycle | Path of vertices where the ends are connected (e.g. 1-2-3-1). |
| Isolated | An unconnected vertice. |
| Line | An infinite series of adjoined points defining a length or arc. |
| Multi-edges | A vertice with multiple edges connecting to another vertice. |
| Path | Series of connected vertices. |
| Point | A location in space typically defined by coordinates, e.g. $(x, y)$, $(x, y, z)$, or $(\rho, \theta)$. When applied to a polygon or polyhedron, points are typically given for vertices. In mathematics a point has no dimension in itself. |
| Polygon | The geometric, two-dimensional shape resulting from connecting vertices. |
| Polyhedron | The topological, three-dimensional shape resulting from connecting vertices. |
| Regular | All vertices have same number of joints. |
| Simple | Graph with no loops nor multi-edges. |
| Simple Cycle | Simple path passing through each vertice. |

| Sparse | Most vertices have few joints. |
| --- | --- |
| Strongly Connected | Paths are always directed. |
| Traveling Salesman | Also called a TSP or Traveling Salesman Problem. Given a series of points to travel among, what is the shortest route to take without passing through each vertice more than once? The problem only sounds easy but becomes increasingly complex based on the dispersion of points. |
| Tree | Undirected paths connected at the ends. |
| Undirected | Quality of an edge or group of edges where the relationship is equally bi-directional (they are each other's "friends") |
| Vertice | A point in space that may be connected to other points by two or more lines; denoted with a V. |
| Weighted | Quality of a graph whereby the edges have distinctive values (e.g. lengths). |

### *Sorting*

| Bubble or Sequential | A "brute force" method good for small lists and with parallel computers that can divide the list. The technique compares the first two values and puts them in order, then compares the third and fourth, etc. After one pass over the numbers, the last value in the list is the highest. The routine then can be repeated without having to check the last value and recurses on itself until all values have been ordered. |
| --- | --- |
| Insertion | Method best suited if list is already close to ordered. The method examines all values in the list except the first. Instead of simply swapping sequentially, it will take the added step of comparing the lesser value with the next value to the left also. For example: 2404, 8653, 1354, 5781 requires two cycles of the algorithm. |
| Quicksort | Divides the search set into two groups then compares values on opposite sides of the median to determine if they are greater or lesser than the median. Those lesser or switched to the left, those greater are switched to the right. The two halves are then treated separately in the same manner and so on until all values have been sorted. Invented by C.A.R. Hoare and published in 1962. It is a recursive function that is faster than any other algorithm, best suited for large sorts. |
| Radix | Sorts by bucketing the values rather than comparing them. Buckets may then be further subdivided or have another algorithm applied to them to complete the sort process. Good for dividing up a list across multiple processors that will then do bubble sorts or other methods. |
| Selection | Searches for then identifies the lowest valued item and inserts it in the first place, then repeats the process confining the array to the remainder until all values are sorted. This is a particularly tedious process |
| Shell | Variation of the insertion sort invented by D.L. Shell. It is a series of insertion sorts that compare values at fixed distances rather than adjacent values. The skip count is reduced with each pass until it reaches one. This saves a lot of time lost with the conventional insertion sort. |

### *Searching*

| Binary | Divides ordered search items in half then determines whether search value is greater or lesser, then repeats the process until the item is found. This is the best method when data can be diagrammed as a binary. |
| --- | --- |
| Insertion | Arranges items so last item is the search item. |
| Sequential | Starts at beginning and tests equality of items until search item is found. Although this algorithm is the simplest to construct, it is the most time consuming and should be reserved for small unordered lists. |
| Sorted | Arranges items until location is found then inserts search item. |

# Worksheet 6—Problem Solving

## RAM

| | | | |
|---|---|---|---|
| a. | Big O Notation | 1. | All computations of speed are ... to language qualities, coding style, and environment |
| b. | LAN or WAN | 2. | The limitations of the programmer in coding that affect speed, not the algorithm. |
| c. | Random Access Machine | 3. | Method of symbolically showing graph relationships between algorithms |
| d. | Relative | 4. | Requires at least Web Design model, most likely combined with Program model |
| e. | Technique | 5. | Used to determine the processing speed of an algorithm |

## Factors Affecting All Programming

| | | | |
|---|---|---|---|
| a. | Data Access | 6. | Composite of parts conditional on information being processed |
| b. | Interface | 7. | It is best to keep this at a minimum in 4th and 5th generation languages |
| c. | Loops | 8. | Less user friendly means faster processing |
| d. | Non-native Code | 9. | May be maximized by carefully defining and organizing the layout |
| e. | Size | 10. | Significant factor when considering resources but not necessarily the rate of algorithm solution |

## Speed Computation

| | | | |
|---|---|---|---|
| a. | $+, -, =, *$ | 11. | A speed so slow that past twenty items the process exceeds life expectancy. |
| b. | cycles/item | 12. | Add each instance to memory calls for a set: divide by number of items in the set to calculate the rate. |
| c. | $n!$ | 13. | Another slow speed that increases geometrically with the number of items. |
| d. | $C\ n \log n$ | 14. | The rate which can be equated to a function describing n to project other rates. |
| e. | $n^2$ | 15. | A fast function because the speed accelerates with more items. |

## Speed Comparison

16. Little o—$f(n)$ ultra fast
17. Big O—$f(n)$ very fast
18. Big Omega ($\Omega$)—$f(n)$ Slow
19. Little Omega ($\omega$)—$f(n)$ ultra slow
20. Theta ($\Theta$)—$f(n)$ faster but parallel potentially equivalent with some coding changes

## Thinking

| | | | |
|---|---|---|---|
| a. | Reasoning | 21. | Logic deriving observed values from specific formulas |
| b. | Rational | 22. | Logic deriving specific formulas from observed values |
| c. | Inductive | 23. | Logical thought independent of moral structure |
| d. | Deductive | 24. | Logical thought within a moral structure |
| e. | Paradigm | 25. | Illustration of a working solution to a class of problems |

## Elements of Thought | Elements of Value

| | | | | | | | |
|---|---|---|---|---|---|---|---|
| | | 26. | Absolutely everything at once | 31. | How manipulation occurs including the environment and available resources | a. | Affective |
| a. | Concrete | 27. | Apply presentational symbols to objects | | | b. | Effective |
| b. | Reflection | 28. | Develop relationships among the presentational objects | 32. | The greatest possible value | c. | Effectual |
| c. | Abstract | | | 33. | The least possible value | d. | Analytical |
| d. | Concept | 29. | Observe the properties of the representational data objects | 34. | The nature of the output | e. | Speculative |
| e. | Holistic | | | 35. | What values are manipulable | | |
| | | 30. | Receive data (representational) objects | | | | |

## Elements of a Problem

| | | | |
|---|---|---|---|
| a. | Foundational (Holistic) | 36. | What exists? |
| b. | Functional (Paradological) | 37. | How do we measure things? |
| c. | Fundamental (Axiological) | 38. | What things do we measure? |
| d. | Formulative (Epistemological) | 39. | What do we know about this and everything else? |
| e. | Facilitative (Metaphysical) | 40. | What do we have when we put it all together? |

## Graph Qualities

41. A length connecting two points
42. A length that only goes one way
43. A length whose distance is significant
44. A point or node on a graph
45. A reciprocal length
46. Measures degree or direction of relationship

a. Directed
b. Edge
c. Undirected
d. Vertice
e. Weighted

## Describing Intersects

47. All have same number of joints
48. Group of vertices bound as a subset by joining edges
49. Most vertices have few joints
50. Most vertices have many joints
51. Number of edges intersecting (joining) a vertice

a. Degree
b. Dense
c. Regular
d. Sparse
e. Clique

## Identifying Value Qualities

52. Graph with no loops nor multiedges
53. More than one edge connecting the same pair of vertices
54. Series of connected vertices
55. Shortest cycle

a. Girth
b. Multiedges
c. Path
d. Simple

## Identifying Groups

56. Having no directed cycles
57. Path of vertices where the ends are connected (e.g. 1-2-3-1)
58. Simple path passing through each vertice
59. Undirected paths not connected at the ends
60. Undirected paths connected at an end

a. Tree
b. Forest
c. Hamiltonian Cycle
d. Acyclic
e. Simple Cyde

## Connectivity

61. An unconnected vertice
62. Connected vertice in disconnected sets
63. Deleting disconnects graph
64. Paths are always directed
65. Two vertices share an edge

a. Articulation Vertex
b. Connected
c. Connected Component
d. Isolated
e. Strongly Connected

## Adjacency ...

66. Array of pointers used to show connectivity between vertices
67. Illustration of vertice connections
68. n x n array of Boolean values showing connectivity
69. Recommended for most applications

a. Graph
b. List
c. Matrix

## Graph Traversal (Searching for & Finding Things)

70. Arranges items so last item is the search item
71. Arranges items until location is found then inserts search item
72. Divides ordered search items in half then determines whether search value is greater or lesser, then repeats the process until the item is found.
73. Starts at beginning and tests equality of items until search item is found.

a. Binary
b. Insert
c. Sequential
d. Sorted

## Finish the Partial Graph

74. β
75. ζ
76. ε
77. ι
78. ν

**79-83**

Describe
the path
to γ.

**Greek Alphabet (in order)**

1. α      14. ξ
2. β      15. ο
3. γ      16. π
4. δ      17. ρ
5. ε      18. φ
6. ζ      19. σ
7. η      20. τ
8. θ      21. υ
9. ι      22. φ
10. κ    23. χ
11. λ    24. ψ
12. μ    25. ω
13. ν

## Identifying Graphs

83. Undirected
79. Tree
80. Simple Cyde
81. Multiedges
82. Directed

83. In B
α:β & Γ:Δ are
a. Reciprocal
b. Loops
c. Cyclic
d. Simple

84. In D use a
_____ search
algorithm:
a. Sorted
b. Binary
c. Sequential
d. Insert

| Error in Table | 85. There is an error In the table below. Identify it. |
|---|---|

**Table in Illustration**

86. Identify the values that should appear in the cells as 0 or 1:
   a. ____
   b. ____
   c. ____
   d. ____
   e. ____

**Identify the Table**

87. The table illustrates what method of showing relationships between vertices?

**Identify the Graph**

88. What qualities does a graph like this have?

_____

_____

|   | A | C | M | P | S | T |
|---|---|---|---|---|---|---|
| **A** | 1 | 0 | 0 | 1 | 1 | 0 |
| **C** | 0 | 1 | 1 | 1 | 1 | 1 |
| **M** | 0 | 1 | 1 | 1 | 1 | 0 |
| **P** | 1 | A | 1 | 1 | D | 0 |
| **S** | 1 | B | 1 | 1 | 1 | E |
| **T** | 0 | C | 0 | 0 | 0 | 0 |

**Computing Relationships**

89. What formula could calculate adjoining edges using the table alone? Would this work based on the graph (i.e. accounting for multiedges)?

**Degree**

90. If this were a friendship graph, how many edges adjoin Mesa?

**Construct a list illustrating the graph**

Example:     A—P—S

91.     C—

92.     M—

93.     P—

94.     S—

95.     T—

## RAM Activity:
### 1-5 identify the sequence of the common factorial algorithm (g(n)):

| Factorial ( ) | | | | |
|---|---|---|---|---|
| private integer n = Input; | | 1. _____ | return n; | |
| if n == 0   {   **A**   } | | 2. _____ | return n * FactorialRecurseOld (n - 1); | |
| if n < 0 \|\| n != Input | | | | |
|         {   **B**   } | | 3. _____ | return FormulaFailure ("Cannot compute negative values nor fractions."); | |
| else      {   **C**   } | | | | |
| FactorialRecurseOld ( ) | | 4. _____ | return FactorialRecurseOld (n); | |
| if n == 1  {   **D**   } | | | | |
| else       {   **E**   } | | 5. _____ | n = 1; | |

### 6-12 identify the sequence of the new factorial algorithm ($f(n)$):

| | |
|---|---|
| A.   if n == 0         // Allows calculation of 0, retains imaginary part (1 - 4 cycles)<br>      {<br>      n = 1;<br>      ZeroFactorial = (-1);<br>      } | 6. _____<br><br>7. _____ |
| B.   n = FactorialRecurse (n);     // Assigns calculation results for n to n (1 cycle) | |
| C.   FactorialRecurse ( )// Calculates the series in 4n-2 cycles (note n=1 when input=0)<br>      if n ◯ 1<br>      {<br>      return n;<br>      }<br>      else<br>      {<br>      counter + +;<br>      return n * FactorialRecurse (n - 1);<br>      } | 8. _____<br><br>9. _____<br><br>10. _____<br><br>11. _____<br><br>12. _____ |
| D.   Factorial ( )           // Initiation of variables (4 cycles)<br>      Private integer neg = 1;<br>      Private float n = FactorialInput;<br>      Public integer ZeroFactorial = 1;<br>      Private integer counter = 0; | |
| E.   return neg * n;        // Provides final results in 1 cycle | 13. Argument is:<br>    a.   ==<br>    b.   >= |
| F.   if counter % 2 == 0 // Provides positive results for even computations (3 - 5 cycles)<br>      {<br>      neg * = neg;<br>      } | c.   !=<br>    d.   <= |
| G.       if n < 0            // Remembers and removes initial negative (1 - 5 cycles)<br>          {<br>                   neg = (-1);<br>                   n * = neg;<br>          } | 14. -2.2! = _____<br>    a.   .528<br>    b.   -.528<br>    c.   4.84<br>    d.   -4.84 |

## RAM Graphed:

15. Valid input for the common factorial (top g(n)) takes _____ cycles per unit of n to compute.
16. Valid input for the new factorial ($f$(n)) > 0 takes an average of _____ cycles per unit of n to compute.
17. This is an example of _____ notation for ($f$(n))?

   **A.** o   **B.** O   **C.** Ω   **D.** ω   **E.** Θ

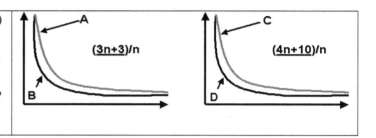

# Unit 7—Database Design

## Objectives

This material was designed for a three contact-hour period in a junior-senior level Algorithms course. It may prove very useful for students seriously considering programming. In this supplemental chapter, students will learn:

| | |
|---|---|
| 1. Database Objects | 4. Normalizing (MCSD) |
| 2. Field Design | 5. Relationships (MCSD) |
| 3. Data Type, Field Size and Input Masks | 6. Computer Math Concepts |

I recommend ~~reading~~ memorizing(!) this entire chapter before you create any table. This information does not fit into a neat sequence, but it is all necessary to understanding table design. Most of this is also critical to the MCSD.

## General Terms

Batch: Processing information in groups as opposed to transaction processing (randomly and singularly). Reports and queries are typically processed in batches, while the data entry for records and expressions are processed by the transaction.

Consider a table with a field labeled "Age," with the data type being number. By using a number you can create an "expression," which is the same as building a formula. Enter birth dates in one field and use an expression to calculate the current age so the age field never needs to be manually updated. The expression will need to link to a field containing the current date (available under the Insert menu as Date and Time).

Data Access (ability to retrieve and use data) Database: A collection of data related to a particular topic or purpose; a table comprised of group of records containing fields of categorized information. A collection of related files stored together that allow you to define relationships between those files so multiple files may be simultaneously accessed. Programs other than databases use a "flat file" meaning each record is separate and self-contained (e.g. not related to the other files directly).

Data Acquisition (inputting and importing) Data Accuracy (of input or import) or data integrity refers to the reliability of the data and that the data is reported and entered correctly. Timely data has not lost its usefulness or legitimacy because of the passage of time.

Data Maintenance (updating, sorting) is the procedures used to keep data current (see accuracy above), such as updating. Data maintenance procedures may overlap data security procedures to also include file management activities and backups.

Data Management: The procedures used to acquire, access and maintain data. Ensures that data required for an application will be available in the correct form and at the proper time for processing.

Data Security (accessibility of users to specific information) protects data from being misused or lost. Part of data security is Backup, where files are copied and stored in the event of extraneous circumstances (e.g. disasters: manmade, natural, or with the system).

Data Type: As with a spreadsheet, the database allows you to define data types such as text, number, date/time, etc. You may have one or more fields that contain graphics, such as company logos. The database also allows you to perform calculations using "expressions."

Expression: An expression uses the field names to perform calculations within a record. In the table view of the records, expressions in the database may be constructed similar to formulas in a spreadsheet.

Query-by-example (QBE): helps you to construct a query by displaying a list of fields that are available in the files, in which you enter known information and prompt to provide all records containing the values you entered in the query fields. Hoover's Master List uses this query method. Note: typically this format is previously specified.

Querying: Creates views and report content and layout. Allows you to retrieve information from the database based on specified criteria in a format previously specified or one that you specify.

Realtime: The computer equivalent of Just-In-Time and FIFO (First In First Out). The information is processed as it is presented to the system. Form use is processed in real time (e.g. changing record information).

Relational Querying: Allows you to query and manipulate data to create a unique view or subset of the total data. Uses relational operators to specify search criteria and perform manipulations, such as select, project and join. Select finds specific records, project specifies the fields within the records that appear in the output, and join combines files/tables for an integrated query which is typically saved in a separate file for future use.

Report: A layout of information intended to be printed or viewed. This layout will be standardized like a form, making it easy to find desired information at a glance. Often, in industry, forms will already be designed and standardized. This is convenient because then you do not have to manually layout the form. If the form does not already exist, then it may be necessary to examine the information going into the form first, to be sure that the layout and the "shape" of the output are not in conflict.

Structured Query Language (SQL pronounced see-qwell): Now a common language used to write relational queries; typically available in most database programs. Allows for more complicated querying and reporting where decisions are necessary (e.g. where . . . = . . . replaces BASIC operations like if . . . then, or for . . . and simplifies these with "and" statements to allow for multiple conditions to be necessary for an action to occur).

## Advantages of Using a Database

Reduced redundancy: data does not need to be duplicated nor entered more than once. The information is stored once, retrieved and used as needed for various applications. The process of splitting tables or merging tables to make better use of data space and reduce redundancy is called **normalization**.

Improved accuracy: reduced redundancy means less chances of error. If there is an error, it needs correcting only once to be reflected in all applications of the data.

Easier reporting: retrieves only the information needed by using a query, so information may be acquired from multiple files simultaneously.

Improved security: allows for various levels of data accessibility, such as not allowing access, allowing read-only access, and "full update" privileges (e.g. edit or read and write access).

Reduces production time: Not only is less time used for data entry, developing programs that access the data is easier as is updating or changing the database program being used. New files need not be created, when new records may be added or fields added to existing records.

Note: It is easy to overlook the fact that it is easier to deal with information consistently entered. It is also easier to reduce the amount of information than to add to the information. For example, a series of records storing responses to surveys should contain all information provided on the surveys even if they are not currently in use. This prevents having to later add new fields to the data and try to accurately enter the data at a later time.

## Database Qualities

Data Dictionary (definitions of fields such as field shape, name, description, type of data, default value, validation rules, and the relationship to other data elements)

Utility Program (creates files and dictionaries, monitors performance, copies data, and deletes unwanted records)

Security (controls levels of access to data)

Replication (Distributes data to other computers to update remote computer databases, typically for purposes of having a central database from which information is updated, while distributing only the necessary information to remote computers)

Recovery (restores information after equipment failure) Sophisticated databases often keep a log of what the database had before and after a change was made (before and after image). "Forward recovery" or "rollforward" automatically reenters the changes made at the time of the last backup. "Backward recovery" or "rollback" reverses the changes that occurred over a specified period of time, which requires all transactions during that time be reentered.

Query Language (creates views and report content and layout) Allows you to retrieve information from the database based on specified criteria in a format you specify.

## Database Types

Hierarchical—Organizes data in a series like a tree. The highest-ranking parent record is called a root record. From the root record is derived the parent records, which accesses the child records. Each child record can have only one parent record (a record that accesses the information within the record lower in hierarchy)

Hierarchy of Data—The various levels of the data (bit, byte, field, record, file/table, relational database. The order (from lowest to highest) is:

Bit—binary digit of 0 for off and 1 for one

Byte—a single character or unit of information stored in a quantity of bits (8, 16, 32, etc.)

Field—Individual elements of descriptive data consisting of one or more characters or units (e.g. bytes)

Record—A group of related fields combined to describe a single person, place, thing, etc.

File/Table—A group of related records that share field attributes but not necessarily the contents of the fields.

Relational Database—A set of related files/tables grouped to perform functions interactively between the records of separate tables and their respective fields.

Network—Allows multiple sources (parents) to access and modify members (children) similar to a hierarchy.

Relational Database—A collection of one or more related tables that can share information. The tables are related to each other and are thus called "relations." The relations, like tables, are divided into rows called "tuples," and fields called "attributes". The range of available field/attribute values is called the "domain".

Object-Oriented—Contains both data and actions (expressions) for managing the data, such as instructions on how to display or print the data, calculation methods, etc.

## Database Objects

Databases have a variety of object types, which are listed below. Each object name should have no spaces, and the first letter of each word in a name is capitalized, or an underline (_) is used to separate the words. The naming conventions listed in the table below may be placed either in front of the object name (TBLMyName) or after (MyNameTBL). I prefer to put the naming convention after so I can see related objects together when viewing them all. Note also that I use additional conventions to help create categories of objects, which I identify as we discuss the objects.

| Object Type | Convention | Description |
|---|---|---|
| Table | TBL | A layout of raw information in columns and rows where a row represents a record and a column represents a field where information is stored to define a record. In Access the field "shape" includes input masks, field sizes, formatting, and data types, which will restrict data input. |
| Query | QRY | Queries either acquire and manipulate information from one or more tables based on criteria (select queries) or perform a function (action queries), such as updating records, deleting records, creating a table, or appending records from one table to another. The viewable results of a select query always look like a table. |
| Form | FRM | A graphical layout of fields whose source is either a tale or a query. Forms limit the user's access to data and provide a means for the programmer to include meaningful descriptions and create a path of travel for the user to put data in correctly. |
| Report | RPT | A printout of information derived from a table or query. |
| Macro | MCR | A sequential set of instructions to perform specific actions (like closing and opening things) that can be applied to any object in a form. In Access these are remarkably easy to do, and will be discussed in detail later. See Trigger below. |

| Module | MOD | A Visual Basic for Applications (VBA) program used to perform special functions. I recommend using these sparingly if at all, and have not personally found a good use for them if you are capable with query and macro design. However, when analyzing your database, the wizard may recommend compiling forms and macros into modules. If so, then I recommend following the directions given after you are certain you will make no further modifications. This way you can rest assured that the coding is absolutely correct. Anyone who has done manual coding in any language understands the hardships of even the slightest human error and can appreciate letting the application program itself. For the MCSD you must understand the concept of a **Trigger**. A **trigger** is an event (insertion, update, or deletion) executing a stored procedure. The stored procedures in Access can be either macros or modules. |
|--------|-----|-----------------------------------------------------------------------------------------|

## Planning a Database

You will note that the list provided here contains different steps and a slightly different order from lists in other books. It also appears to be in reverse order of what one might think to do. This is a practical application oriented approach, meaning you first determine the end product then design the means of accomplishing that product. Furthermore, this list does not neglect the fact that another database program or system may be more appropriate than Access. For example, the size of the database may be such that it is not practical for Access (take AltaVista's database of indexed web pages as an example).

Design the structure of the reports you want to be able to generate from the database, including the necessary fields of information and their shapes, as well as any extraneous information (e.g. headers and footers or other text or graphics that will appear on each form). Design the structure of the records, defining the fields, their data types, and any "expressions" in which a field will provide an automatically calculated value.

Determine the purpose of the database (e.g. What will the database represent (item b)? What will it be used to do (item a)? How large will the database be?). Note that the size of the database may also play a factor in hardware requirements, such as available disk space, RAM, and processor speed.

Determine what type of database or what database program is most appropriate to fit the desired purpose (e.g. for reporting and querying). Find the simplest means of importing or entering the desired information necessary to the database (e.g. importing from various spreadsheets, word processor created lists, etc.). If you are importing data, it is essential to be sure the data is in a manageable format before attempting to import it to your database.

Gather together all the forms, which will be filled out/generated from the data in the database. Identify the various fields of information contained within the forms

Separate the various fields into appropriate groups that should be stored in separate tables (files).

Using the fields of one group, design the File on paper first (or use an existing form) containing all the fields necessary to that group.

Include a unique key field, like a record number or account number.

Use separate fields for logically distinct items. Typically it is wise to have separate fields for first, middle and last names, title, company name, phone number, fax, e-mail, URL, street address, post office box, city, state/state code, zip code, and four digit zip code extension. Note: State and state code are not the same. If you wish the state name to be spelled out and to have the code, it may be wise to have separate fields for each.

Do not create fields that can be derived from entries in other fields.

Allow enough space for the information (the shape of the field). Foreign addresses, names and phone numbers may require extra space. Shape: The dimensions of a field required to show the data. If the data is to be printed on fixed shape forms, then the shape of each field must clearly defined providing a limit to the quantity of information (number of characters) that may be stored in that field. If the data is to be viewed electronically, then the shape is governed more by cosmetics (for most practical viewing) and the size limitations of the database.

Create default values for frequently entered data (e.g. the state when most records will be in the same state). Note: It is unwise to require a field have an entry especially if the entry is not appropriate. For example, state code will not apply for foreign addresses, so allow for blank spaces.

Implement your design and input the data.

## Field Design

The following guidelines assume that you follow the other rules defined in this chapter (and there are many!). As such, when I say something like "Include a unique key..." I mean if that key is appropriate according to the rules of normalization, lookups, indexing and key fields. Sound like a handful? That is why database designers make a lot of money and hackers pay developers a fortune to rebuild failing databases.

1. Gather together all the forms, which will be filled out/generated from the data in the database.
2. Identify the various fields of information contained within the forms
3. "Normalize" or "atomize" these fields so an information field is only identified once (First Normal Form). It is typically seen as easier to combine information (denormalize) than to separate it (normalize). Always reduce first to the lowest denominator then denormalize for functionality and to balance system resources. For example, on a gradebook database, I first atomized assignment entry into two fields, the first containing a lookup to different types of assignments and the second to name the type selected. I related these two to the student grades and everything looked all right until I tried tracking a class. Then I could only see what the assignment type was, not the title, so I denormalized (merged) the fields and eliminated the lookup. Sometimes less is more. Limit the user only when absolutely necessary to ensure proper functionality.
4. Separate the various fields into appropriate groups that should be stored in logically separate tables.
5. Using the fields of one group, design the table on paper first (or use an existing form) containing all the fields necessary to that group:
   a. Include a unique key field, like a record number or account number if the table will be a parent table.
   b. Use separate fields for logically distinct items. Typically it is wise to have separate fields for first, middle and last names, title, company name, phone number, fax, e-mail, URL, street address, post office box, city, state/state code, zip code, and four digit zip code extension. Note: State and state code are not the same. If you wish the state name to be spelled out and to have the code, it may be wise to have separate fields for each.
   c. Do not create fields that can be derived from entries in other fields (e.g. from expressions that can be created in queries).
   d. Allow enough space for the information (the shape of the field). Foreign addresses, names and phone numbers may require extra space. Shape: The dimensions of a field required to show the data. If the data is to be printed on fixed shape forms, then the shape of each field must clearly defined providing a limit to the quantity of information (number of characters) that may be stored in that field. If the data is to be viewed electronically, then the shape is governed more by cosmetics (for most practical viewing) and the size limitations of the database.
   e. Define data types, formatting, input masks and indexing qualities
   f. Create necessary lookups
   g. Create default values for frequently entered data (e.g. the state when most records will be in the same state). I discourage the use of default data as it can result in data-entry errors that are extremely difficult to track which result from oversight and laziness. It is easier to find and repair data errors if a field is accidentally left blank than if it is automatically filled.
   h. Create validation rules and other data entry rules. It is unwise to require a field have an entry especially if the entry is not appropriate. For example, state code will not apply for foreign addresses, so allow for blank spaces.
6. Repeat step 5 until all tables are developed necessary to accomplish the desired results.
7. Create input and output mediums (these are potentially interchangeable and may even be worked simultaneously at times):

Worksheet 6—Problem Solving
Unit 7—Database Design

      a.    Create queries to perform desired computations (expressions) and present the data required for the forms in step 1.
      b.    Create reports to print out the desired information.
      c.    Create a user interface (Form objects, macros and modules) to insure proper data entry.
8.    Develop security measures to limit user access to data and design.
9.    Test all features of the design with sufficient data to potentially break the system (e.g. normal operating conditions) on the least capable users with no training (particularly those known to break things without trying) and observe the consequences. I know it sounds cruel to those users, but if they can use it and not break it, then it will likely do well under real pressure. Often tests are run using the most competent users. From a management perspective this means lost production time with their most valued employees. Personally, as a manager, I would rather risk losing production time on already unproductive employees because I stand to gain productivity from them if the system actually works. Note: Microsoft justifiably recommends aiming development at company regulation levels and not the lowest known denominator. I would argue you should fill both objectives, because failure to do so means your project is not justified because the existing system clearly did not work. If the system had worked, your project would never be considered.

## *Primary Field Attributes*

### Field Names
Access will allow you to create long field names with spaces in them. Do not abuse length, and definitely do not put spaces into your field names. While these practices are alright with dysfunctional database designs, they are dysfunctional because eventually the developer hacks their way into a feature that does not forgive the spaces (like real programming). It is wise to have a naming convention that is brief, intuitive and logical. It is also wise to try avoiding using the same field names in other tables as this could become confusing for you, and more disastrously, could confuse the programming code of a SQL statement or module. Field names <u>must</u> be unique within a table, and <u>should</u> be unique among the field names of the other tables in the database. If you want the user to see a name other than the field name, change the Caption attribute on the General tab at the bottom of the Table design view.

### Constraints and Validation (MCSD)
Constraints limit what kind of data can be entered into an field or table (often called an entity on the MCSD), how the data is entered, and the order in which the data is entered. One way to control the order data is entered in is to follow the **Navigation Model**, which defines how the user navigates through the interface (for Access this often means switchboards, action buttons and forms).
Note: this paragraph is crucial for the MCSD. Types of validation include Point-of-Entry (forces the user to make input), Field Level (tests validity when field is updated, but before stored data is updated), Transaction Level (when the record is going to be updated). Validation occurs at one of the following points: when a field is updated or modified (the user types or edits field contents), when a record is deleted, and when a record is updated. Access automatically validates information based on data types (when field goes to update), input masks (as you type), key field (these are automatically required and must be different from each other, occurs typically when the record is updated), and relationships (when you try to delete or modify something that is related to something else). You can go beyond the defaults of Access and otherwise require a field and/or provide a default value. I do not encourage the use of default values as they can lead to quality assurance nightmares. It is much easier to get information than to wade through misinformation that is default and verify it all.
You can set more validation rules by using the ValidationRule property. If you set the ValidationRule property but not the ValidationText property, Microsoft Access displays a standard error message when the validation rule is violated. If you set the ValidationText property, the text you enter is displayed as the error message in a message box. All rules created in the Table design (including error message boxes, masks, etc.) are also applied in forms even if the form is indirectly derived through a query. If your tables are from external sources (e.g. dBASE, Paradox, or a SQL server) you cannot modify table properties, so you can only apply rules to controls on your forms (independent of the table).

Control, field, and record validation rules are applied as follows:

- Validation rules you set for fields and controls are applied when you edit the data and the focus leaves the field or control.
- Validation rules for records are applied when you move to another record.
- If you create validation rules for both a field and a control bound to the field, both validation rules are applied when you edit data and the focus leaves the control.

The following table contains expression examples for the ValidationRule and ValidationText properties.

| ValidationRule property | ValidationText property |
|---|---|
| <> 0 | Entry must be a nonzero value. |
| > 1000 Or Is Null | Entry must be blank or greater than 1000. |
| Like "A????" | Entry must be 5 characters and begin with the letter "A". |
| >= #1/1/96# And <#1/1/97# | Entry must be a date in 1996. |
| DLookup("CustomerID", "Customers", "CustomerID = Forms!Customers!CustomerID") Is Null | Entry must be a unique CustomerID (domain aggregate functions are allowed only for form-level validation). |

To allow a Null value, add "Is Null" to the validation rule, as in "<> 8 Or Is Null" and make sure the Required property is set to No.

**Formatting and Descriptions**

Formatting is only a visual constraint and does not directly affect the data. As a consequence forcing upper case characters with a > in the Format field on the General card succeeds in generating programmer headaches because case sensitive searches will fail. As such, I discourage considering formatting as a constraint, but rather consider it a visual bonus to help the user correctly recognize information. Note: to show the date as 01/01/1901 use the format mm/dd/yyyy, which will prevent numeric conflicts between dates early in the twentieth and twenty-first centuries. Another useful formatting mask is HH:MM:SS AM for times.

Likewise, descriptions and tooltips are only useful if the user notices them. Descriptions appear in the status bar, giving users and programmers additional information to help understand the field. Most likely the person who reads descriptions is already an advanced user and will not need the extra information. I recommend using forms with descriptive labels and help files that are easily found and used. Likewise, new users are likely to move the mouse too quickly to get tooltips, but when they finally slow down these act as comments in other documents which can be immensely helpful as context-sensitive help. You might put a "Quick Help" button on your form that produces a message box that reads "For quick help on a specific item, point your mouse pointer at the field and leave it there until a tooltip appears." Then provide descriptive tooltip information for each field shown on the form.

## Data Type, Field Size and Input Masks

Data type greatly inhibits user mistakes, as data entry is halted by system errors when the user enters data not supported by the data type. After choosing the data type (see the table below), be sure the field size is appropriate. For example, although personal names can get long, I doubt you will have any problem identifying a first or last name, or a city name in 20 characters. Likewise you should never need more than fifty characters to identify the name of a company or the street address. Finally, field size can be affected by the input mask., which may or may not specify storing constant characters with the data (e.g. with phone numbers, social security numbers and business tax ID numbers, all you really need are the numbers, the rest is just for looks; however...if you are storing individuals in the same table as companies you may not want to use an input mask at all because their numbers are presented differently!). The following tables will help put all this together more meaningfully.

## Data Type

| Data Type | Description |
|---|---|
| Text | Supports up to 255 characters. The default when designing a table from scratch is 50. The default when you import a table from another application (e.g. text or Excel) is 255. I personally find no good reason to exceed 50 as this is a large amount of space to risk leaving vacant. If you exceed 50 you are likely to need more than 255, meaning you should use the Memo type or hyperlink. |
| Memo | This field should be used in reservation as it is difficult to apply in reports and can take up a lot of space. Use this type for fields where you expect more than 255 characters. When information gets this verbose, it should probably be broken into paragraphs and have formatting features applied meaningfully. As such I recommend using the hyperlink type to create hyperlinks to other documents (e.g. Word, Excel, PowerPoint, etc.). Memo supports up to 64,000 characters. |
| Number | For all real numbers (see field size table below). If you need decimal values be sure to select the appropriate data type (single, double, and decimal) and specify the number of decimal places you want (otherwise all numbers are treated as integers, which are whole numbers). |
| Date/Time | For all dates and times, which is really a numeric value applied to a formatting style showing the date or time. You must use this data type if you wish to use the field for calculations. See Formatting above for more information on customizing your date beyond the selections available. |
| Currency | As the name suggests, this type stores numbers (up to 15 digits to the left of the decimal and 4 to the right of the decimal). It consumes 8 bytes, so you might consider a different data type with formatting applied instead (see Number) |
| AutoNumber | Produces an automatically generated, sequential number. Commonly used for a key field when there is no other useful number available. Always defaults to a Long Integer field size, and should be left that way. A problem with autonumbers is that once a number is used it is never reused in the same table. As a consequence when you put in sample data you will reduce the number of available records in the table by the number of sample records you test. For this reason it is preferable to use a meaningful number like social security number, part number, etc. as they can be deleted and later reused. Do not worry too much about running out of Long Integer values though because Long Integers go as high as two billion. |
| Yes/No | This is the smallest data type but should still be used conservatively as the user may get confused. It appears as a checkbox. When selected (stores a 1) it indicates the value is true, and when deselected it indicates the value is false (stores a 0). |
| OLE Object | This allows you to to link or embed another document (up to 1 gigabyte!) created by another application. Linked files may be updated by double clicking them then making the modifications in the original application (assuming both are installed properly for both the Windows registry and the location of the file within the system). Embedded objects must be re-embedded if they are modified and will inflate your file size enormously. Personally I would reserve this data type for pictures when you have few pictures to include (e.g. employee photographs). Otherwise I would use the hyperlink type. |
| Hyperlink | Like the memo type, this stores up to 64,000 characters (which I assume includes both the title and link information). This does not mean I would encourage you to use all those characters. Keep it short and sweet, and be careful where you hyperlink to, especially if you expect to move the database or use it across a network. |

| | |
|---|---|
| Lookup... | This type of field provides a combination box for the user to select from a predefined list or from another table (always the same size as the **Primary Key** field referenced from another table (a.k.a. the **Foreign Key**). |

*Field Size*

| Field Size | Description | Decimal precision | Storage size |
|---|---|---|---|
| <number showing> | Defines the number of characters a field can store. | None | Number Shown in bytes |
| Byte | Stores numbers from 0 to 255 (no fractions). | None | 1 byte |
| Integer | Stores numbers from –32,768 to 32,767 (no fractions). | None | 2 bytes |
| Long Integer | (Default) Stores numbers from –2,147,483,648 to 2,147,483,647 (no fractions). | None | 4 bytes |
| Single | Stores numbers from –3.402823E38 to –1.401298E–45 for negative values and from 1.401298E–45 to 3.402823E38 for positive values. | 7 | 4 bytes |
| Double | Stores numbers from –1.79769313486231E308 to –4.94065645841247E–324 for negative values and from 1.79769313486231E308 to 4.94065645841247E–324 for positive values. | 15 | 8 bytes |
| Replication ID | Globally unique identifier (GUID) (See COM Objects) | N/A | 16 bytes |
| Decimal | Stores numbers from -10^38 -1 through 10^38 -1 (.adp) Stores numbers from-10^28 -1 through 10^28 -1 (.mdb) | 28 | 12 bytes |

## Input Masks

Input masks have a very specific layout. The following table defines the qualities of each layout section.

| Mask | Storage | Placeholder |
|------|---------|-------------|
| Specifies the input mask itself; for example, (999) 999-9999. For a list of characters you can use to define the input mask, see the following table. | To stores the literal display characters use 0 for this section. If you leave this blank or use a 1, only typed characters are stored, but not display characters. For example: (999) 999-9999;;_ stores only ten characters (not the parentheses, space nor hyphen). Access will convert this same mask as: \(999\)\ 999\-9999;;_ | Specifies the character displayed for spaces where typing occurs during data entry. For this section, you can use any character. To display an empty string, use a space enclosed in quotation marks (" "). |

To do the same thing in Visual Basic use a string expression to set this property. For example, the following specifies an input mask for a text box control used for entering a phone number:

### Forms!Customers!Telephone.InputMask = "(###) ###-####"

This next table provides the characters used in the mask.

| Character | Description |
|-----------|-------------|
| 0 | Digit (0 to 9, entry required, plus [+] and minus [−] signs not allowed). |
| 9 | Digit (0 to 9) or space (entry not required, plus and minus signs not allowed). |
| # | Digit (0 to 9) or space (entry not required; spaces are displayed as blanks while in Edit mode, but blanks are removed when data is saved; plus and minus signs allowed). |
| L | Letter (A to Z, entry required). |
| ? | Letter (A to Z, entry optional). |
| A | Letter or digit (entry required). |
| a | Letter or digit (entry optional). |
| & | Any character or a space (entry required). |
| C | Any character or a space (entry optional). |
| . , : ; - / | Decimal placeholder and thousand, date, and time separators. (The actual character used depends on the settings in the **Regional Settings Properties** dialog box in Windows Control Panel). |
| < | Causes all characters to be converted to lowercase. Use here and not in Format! |
| > | Causes all characters to be converted to uppercase. Use here and not in Format! |
| ! | Causes the input mask to display from right to left, rather than from left to right. Characters typed into the mask always fill it from left to right. You can include the exclamation point anywhere in the input mask. This is good if you use a mask with a number where the last digits will always be in the same decimal areas (e.g. currency) |
| \ | Causes the character that follows to be displayed as the literal character (for example, \A is displayed as just A). |

**Note** Setting the **InputMask** property to the word "Password" creates a password-entry control. Any character typed in the control is stored as the character but is displayed as an asterisk (*). You use the Password input mask to prevent displaying the typed characters on the screen.

## Lookup Fields

### General Lookups (MCSD)

Lookup fields reduce data entry errors. There are two types of lookup: embedded and linked. An embedded lookup stores the data source in the table design. Use an embedded lookup for a limited list of choices to insure data entry is consistent, such as state names or abbreviations (Note: the Format property > to force upper case is not always reliable when the data is queried). A linked lookup pulls information from another table by way of a **Foreign Key** field. Whenever linking a lookup be sure to have a key field in the source table (this will be the Foreign Key) and to include the key field in the lookup, even if you do not wish to show it. Note: If you are using a linked lookup and want a default value from the source table, use a key field value and not the name that would appear. During data entry you can type the name, but run the risk that other records will have the same name. For this reason it is typically wise to include more than one non-key field in your lookup.

## Lookups to Queries

You can create a linked lookup whose data source is a query. I like to use this **Navigation** tables. Here we will only address the benefits and limitations, reserving the How-To for much later (because this requires good Form, Query and Macro development skills).

*Benefits (and though there are so few, from the end-user's perspective they mean everything):*

1. The choices in the lookup field are limited and potentially more meaningful as they are based on other data you already entered.
2. The choices are sorted how you want them rather than strictly by the key field.

*Limitations:*

1. There are a lot of points where failure is possible in the design.
2. Data entry must be done on a form to prevent errors, macros must be assigned to the appropriate fields, and over all the form design needs careful handling.
3. When looking at the source table, only names current in the query are active, otherwise only the key fields show.
4. If the query is done without a navigation table or without a logical limitation on the results (like active records only), the query will fail.
5. The lookup relationship is with the query and not the source table, and as a consequence forms and subforms derived there from must be based on queries. This itself can also be a benefit if you are good at developing queries.
6. Failure to enforce referential integrity with cascade options selected will be extremely tragic (lost data).
7. The user cannot select something from this field not available in the query. For example, if I have a parent CourseTBL and a child SectionTBL I could create a NavigationTBL with a lookup to the CourseID and another to a query for SectionIDs matching the CourseID. I set my NavigationFRM to reload itself when the CourseID is changed so my query is updated for the SectionIDs. I have no choice but to select a CourseID first, as all other SectionIDs are currently hidden. To help my user I provide a message box activated by a help button that explains, "If the section you are looking for is not listed, be sure the correct Course is selected. If the correct Course is selected go to the General Information form and verify the section exists and add it if necessary."

### *Indexing and Key Fields (MCSD)*

### Indexing

Indexing provides a means for Access to quickly find information. This is particularly important for large databases and databases on networks. Without an index, Access is forced to look for information sequentially, which is extremely time consuming. An index provides ordered numeric values of where information is. Consider a telephone book, where individuals may have multiple phone numbers. If you want to find all the telephone numbers of an individual it is much faster to look them up by name rather than by the phone numbers.

An indexed field is either sorted or unsorted. Access automatically sorts the data when the table or form is closed after data entry by the first field with the index property: Yes (No Duplicates). An unsorted index has the index property: Yes (Duplicates OK). Access retains a list that cannot be seen of the values appearing in a field with this index property along with an unduplicated reference (e.g. record number, key field, or other sorted index) so it can rapidly locate the records.

**Key Fields**

Key fields are always indexed. When there is only one key field then the Index property will be: Yes (No Duplicates). When there are multiple keys then the index property for each will be: Yes (Duplicates OK). When to have a key field:

- To prevent records from being confused with each other
- When the table has a field referenced by a lookup in another table (always include the key field in the lookup!)

Never have a key field on a **Terminal** table (see the schedule.mdb on the Internet) where:

- There are no relationships to other table or
- One or more fields are lookups to other tables and
- The table has no children of its own

## Normalizing (MCSD)

Note: the three entities (Associative, Characteristic, and Kernel) are the terms used in the MCSD <u>Analyzing Requirements and Defining Solutions Architectures</u>.

| | |
|---|---|
| Associative Table (Associative Entity) | A table that derives all of its data from two or more tables, creating a relationship between those tables that could not otherwise exist. Recommended naming conventions: TableNameDetailsTBL, TableNameDTBL, TableNameATBL. |
| Characteristic Table (Characteristic Entity) | A child table providing information about a parent table that has a variable length. Were this data stored in the parent table, it would result in blank fields for many records. For example, in an order entry system you would have an OrderTBL with a child OrderDetailsTBL. The OrderTBL contains general information pertaining to the order, such as who made the order, the date of the order, who is receiving the order, who is getting billed, and where the order is being shipped. The OrderDetailsTBL links to the key fields of the OrderTBL and the ProductsTBL, and lists the quantity ordered. See the Fourth Normal Form. |
| Child Table | A table that derives data from another table. If a child table does not have any children itself, it should not have a key field. |
| Decomposable | Quality of a table indicating that certain fields contain repetitive data better managed if separated into another table and related by key field. Typically decomposable tables have multiple fields that can be distinguished from each other. Names can be repetitive, but do not themselves justify decomposing the table. |
| Flat Table | A table with no key field and no relationships to other tables. |
| Hierarchical | Quality of a system where the parts are organized such that lower ranking parts inherit the qualities of higher ranking parts. Do not confuse the application of this term in this section with a hierarchical database. In a relational database, child tables inherit the qualities of the parent tables, and child tables provide either variable length characteristic or historical details about the parent table. |
| History Table | A child table whose purpose is to store time-specific data, such as a PriceHTBL or CostHTBL. The data is only applied if the date of the history table corresponds with the related records. See the Tenth Normal Form. Recommended naming conventions: TableNameHistoryTBL, TableNameHTBL |
| Navigation Table | A special function table for which only one record will ever exist. This type of table will be discussed in great detail later. Recommended naming conventions: NavTBL or TableNameNTBL. This is often an associative table, so those naming conventions may also be applied. |
| Normalize | Process of dividing a table into non-decomposable tables. See the Fifth Normal Form. |
| Parent Table | A parent table always contains a key field which is referenced by its children. A parent table could also be a child table if and only if it derives data from another |

| | |
|---|---|
| | table. |
| Primary Table (Kernel Entity) | A parent table with a key field and with no data derived from other tables. A record here provides data describing a singular real-world subject that is not a subset of but rather a superset of other entities. Naming convention: TableNameTBL. |
| Terminal Table | A child table that will not have any children. |

### Terms

| | |
|---|---|
| Child Table | A table that derives data from another table. If a child table does not have any children itself, it should not have a key field. |
| Decomposable | Quality of a table indicating that certain fields contain repetitive data better managed if separated into another table and related by key field. Typically decomposable tables have multiple fields that can be distinguished from each other. Names can be repetitive, but do not justify decomposing the table. |
| Details Table | A child table providing information about a parent table that has a variable length. Were this data stored in the parent table, it would result in blank fields for many records. For example, in an order entry system you would have an OrderTBL with a child OrderDetailsTBL. The OrderTBL contains general information pertaining to the order, such as who made the order, the date of the order, who is receiving the order, who is getting billed, and where the order is being shipped. The OrderDetailsTBL links to the key fields of the OrderTBL and the ProductsTBL, and lists the quantity ordered. See the Fourth Normal Form. |
| Flat Table | A table with no key field and no relationships to other tables. |
| Hierarchical | Quality of a system where the parts are organized such that lower ranking parts inherit the qualities of higher ranking parts. Do not confuse the application of this term in this section with a hierarchical database. In a relational database, child tables inherit the qualities of the parent tables, and child tables provide either variable length details or historical details about the parent table. |
| History Table | A child table whose purpose is to store time-specific data, such as a PriceTBL or CostTBL. The data is only applied if the date of the history table corresponds with the related records. See the Sixth Normal Form. |
| Intersection Table | A table that derives all of its data from two or more tables, creating a relationship between those tables that could not otherwise exist. Recommended naming conventions: TableNameITBL. |
| Navigation Table | A special function table for which only one record will ever exist. This type of table will be discussed in great detail later. Recommended naming conventions: NavTBL or TableNameNTBL. |
| Normalize | Process of dividing a table into non-decomposable tables. See the Fifth Normal Form. |
| Parent Table | A parent table always contains a key field which is referenced by its children. A parent table could also be a child table if and only if it derives data from another table. |
| Primary Table | A parent table with a key field and with no data derived from other tables. |

## Normal Forms

Microsoft provides five "Normal Forms" (see Analyzing Requirements and Defining Solution Architectures for the MCSD) which are rules governing normalizing of relational database design. I faithfully identify these forms first then add my own to the end.

| Form | Definition |
|---|---|
| First | There cannot be decomposable repetitive data among the records of a table. A table violates this rule if one or more fields contain repetitive data that could be stored more concisely in another table using a lookup to the key field of the new table's key field. When designing your tables you should be able to identify repetitive information easily. When this happens, create a new table to store the data in with a key field (typically as an autonumber) and any descriptive fields. Save this table and close it. Return to the original table and create a lookup in a blank available field to the key field. It is also wise to include the name of the record and hide the key field so the user is not confused when they use the lookup during data entry. This can (and should) be done without any data in the tables. |
| Second | According to Microsoft, every field in a table must relate to a primary key field in its entirety (which includes multiple key fields). This rule is typically viewed as a function of multiple key fields (composite key), for which I have added the Eighth Normal Form. The reality of this form, however, is its application to putting the fields in the tables where they belong. For example, a price field belongs in a PriceHTBL (see Tenth Normal Form) not an InvoiceTBL because the price is a function of time and product, not the order. |
| Third | A child table must be related to a parent table through the primary key field. If a composite key is used, this can be a serious problem, because you can only relate to one key field at a time. For this reason I add the Eighth Normal Form. Here, Microsoft is arguing that relating non-key fields in two tables will result in potential data conflicts from many-to-many relationships. Many-to-many relationships occur when a relationship is made between non-key fields (e.g. often without a properly formed lookup). See also the Twelfth through Fourteenth Normal Forms. |
| Fourth | Never create a related field that could be left blank. My recommendation here is to make the lookup field in the child table required. Microsoft's point, however, is that many instances where this might occur are the result of a field that may not always be necessary and should thus be relegated to a **characteristic table**. If the field is not related to another table, then may be a necessary evil. If it is related to another table the practice is forbidden. |

Divide a table into multiple indivisible tables to reduce repetitive data and prevent blank fields.

| | Table | Key | Lookups | Other Fields |
|---|---|---|---|---|
| | StudentTBL | StudentID | | Name, Phone, etc. |
| | CourseTBL | CourseID | | |
| Fifth | TextbookTBL | TextbookID | | Author, Publisher |
| | SectionHTBL | SectionID | CourseID, TextbookID, InstructorID | semester |
| | RosterATBL | RosterID | SectionID, StudentID | |
| | AssignmentCTBL | AssignmentID | SectionID, RosterID | title, value |
| | GradesATBL | | RosterID, AssignmentID | Value |

| Form | Definition |
|---|---|
| Sixth | 1. The fields in a parent table define a key field and do not require a history<br>2. The fields of a child table (which either defines a history, characteristic, or creates an associate), with no key, are definitive of the key fields of the parent tables<br>3. If a child table has a key field (meaning it is also used as a parent), then the fields must fill both 1 and 2 of this form. |
| Seventh | Any table with children must have a single key field. Most typically this is an autonumber if there is no other logical alternative (like a social security number). |

| | |
|---|---|
| Eighth | Never use a composite key. Access allows you to make two more fields share the function of key field. The combination of these fields cannot be repeated. I have found that most instances where composite keys have been established, there should have been no key field at all. Although Microsoft gives you this option, the typical result is a violation of the Second Normal Form. The most likely instigator to inspire multiple key fields is an **Associative table**, which is a child table. If such a child must have children of its own, then follow the Seventh Normal Form. |
| Ninth | Never include a key field in a child table that has no children of its own. |
| Tenth | Typically a terminal table maintaining dated information is a **History** table, which is used to attribute values appropriately to records based on the date of transaction. For example, because prices and costs change over time, history tables should be maintained so reports can be run on old transactions rather than forcing the maintenance of hard copies which become difficult to analyze. This is useful for accounting purposes. |
| Eleventh | Typically a terminal table listing variable amounts of information attributed to a parent table is a **Characteristic table**. In an order entry system, each order can have any number of items associated with the specific order. To account for this variation create an OrderDetailsTBL containing a lookup to the OrderID in the OrderTBL, a lookup to the ProductID (showing the product name) in the ProductTBL and a field indicating the quantity ordered. This example is also an **associative table** as described in the Twelfth Normal Form. An example that fits only this might be a CertificationTBL for instructors, who would have multiple certificates which can be immensely different from each other, and have specific dates of validity. For such a design you would create a lookup from the CertificationTBL to the InstructorID in the InstructorTBL, then provide fields for the granting institution, date awarded, title of the certificate, and the date (if applicable) the certificate expires. |
| Twelfth | Typically a terminal table with lookups to two or more table keys to allow otherwise unrelated tables to be related are **associative tables**. As noted in the Eleventh Normal Form's order entry example, an **associative table** can also contain detail information unique to the association. |
| Thirteen | Never use a key field derived through relationship from another table as a key field in the child table. |
| Fourteen | The combination of lookup fields in an **associative table** must never be repeated. This is an extremely difficult rule because between the Eighth and Thirteenth Normal Forms, it appears impossible to enforce on the user. A solution could be to force the user to enter the fields in a specific order (see Navigation Tables below), and after the first lookup field have each subsequent lookup use a query as its source. Another would be to add a hidden date field with default data of =Now(), create the necessary Delete Query and macros to drive the function to automatically delete the old data when the user replicates. |
| Fifteenth | A terminal table that is an association where only one record can exist in a table and the source data for all fields are lookups to other tables is a **Navigation** table. |

As you can see, my additions provide even greater detail on table design, which often include solutions from other database objects.

### *Hierarchy of Normalized Tables*

To help put this all in perspective, table types are listed in order of relationship priority with brief explanations as to why. I put parents at the top because they provide the most constant, stable data. This is also the order in which you should create your tables.
1.  Flat Tables—not involved in any relationship least affected can be added any time
2.  Parent Tables
    a.  Kernel (Primary Parent) Tables—share data with other tables
    b.  Child tables who are also Parents—both borrow and share data with other tables
3.  Child Tables
    a.  Associative Tables—borrow most or all of their data to regulate complex relationships

b. Other Children—require at least one parent for their data to be meaningful
   - Characteristic Tables
   - History Tables
c. Terminal Tables—potentially descriptive of any child table
d. Navigation Tables—exclusively borrow data as a dominant function for forms and queries

## Relationships (MCSD)

Access is not just a basic database design tool. The database designer should know that Access is limited to 2 million records, but can be attached to a much larger database (e.g. hosted by a SQL server). This is actually common because with the VBA capabilities of Access modules you can create a simple interface with all the simplicities of Access including reports, queries, forms and security without having to reinvent the application and retain the power of a "real" database.

The Access 2000 example has no relationships established in the Relationships Window. **I recommend relationships in the Relationships Window be built only with the Lookup Wizard, then develop other relationships in the queries.** For an example of relationships created with lookups alone see the circular.mdb in the same location on the Internet. All relationships in the example are shown in the queries. Note: if relationships are done in the Relationships Window they will appear in the query when the tables are inserted. You can, however, modify the relationship or even delete it if created in the query alone without affecting the entire database. **I also recommend doing as many expressions as possible in the queries to simplify forms and reports** (not to mention reduce headaches as expressions may work in a report but not in a form and vice-versa).

For fun, redefine the AZcompaniesQRY to prompt for a different state (in the criteria cell type [Please enter the desired state]), then run the other queries choosing other states. The other queries use this as their data source.

### Relationship Types (MCSD)

One-to-One: Both tables have one key field and those key fields are related to each other. This means that a record in one table will only have one matching record in the other table. If such a relationship exists then I recommend merging the tables to simplify the design and reduce the redundancy of listing the same key field twice.

One-to-Many: Both tables have at least on key field and a key field is either related to a non-key field or to a table with multiple keys. For each record in the table with a single key field related to a non-key or multiple key, there are potentially many records in the other table that are related.

Many-to-Many: Both tables are related either with multiple keys or by non-key fields when key fields exist in both. This means a record in either table may have multiple related records in the other. Although Microsoft's Third Normal Form seems to do away with this, **associative tables** defined in the Twelfth through Fourteenth Normal Forms make this possible in a controlled manner.

Undetermined: Neither table contains a key field.

### Join Types (MCSD)

Option 1 (Inner Join)--Shows only matching records of both tables. This is shown by a line with no arrows connecting the related fields.

Option 2 (Right Outer Join)--Shows all records of the "One" table (or if undetermined or many-to-many, the table where you started clicking and dragging) and only matching of the "Many" table (or if undetermined or many-to-many, the table where you release the mouse button). In other words, all the records of the "One" table will show even if there are no matching records in the "Many" table. When there are no matching records in the "Many" table then the requested fields are blank. This is shown by a line connecting the related fields with an arrow pointing to the field in the "Many" table.

Option 3 (Left Outer Join)--Shows all records of the "Many" table (or if undetermined or many-to-many, the table where you release the mouse button) and only matching of the "One" table (or if undetermined or many-to-many, the table where you started clicking and dragging). In other words, all the records of the "Many" table will show even if there are no matching records in the "One" table. When there are no matching records in the "One" table then the requested fields are blank. This is shown by a line connecting the related fields with an arrow pointing to the field in the "One" table. This join type potentially breaks the Third Normal Form unless it is made to a query of the parent table.

Note: Right and Left Outer Joins are visually semantic terms that may be confusing because the direction the arrow is pointing may be reversed simply by moving related tables to the opposite sides of each other. The assumption in data-flow diagramming is that parents (one) will be on the left and children (many) will be on the right. As such, a left outer join would point from the child to the parent. That is why I provide the option number with description as well as the name. To change a left outer join to a right outer join you must double click the joining line and choose the other option. You cannot simply change the location of a table so the arrow physically points left or right to establish the required results.

### Referential Integrity (MCSD)

The rules of referential integrity (when enforcement is selected) are:

- You cannot change a key field referenced **from or by** another table. Note: you can never change a key field referenced from another table because this would damage the records in the child table being edited.
- You cannot change data in a field referenced **from** another table.
- You cannot delete records referenced **by** another table.

To violate these use the options: Cascade Update Related Fields or Cascade Delete Related Records with extreme caution!

When referential integrity is established it can be seen in the Relationship design area of a query or in the Relationships Window by the ones (1) and infinites ($\infty$) indicating which table is "One" (1) versus "Many" ($\infty$). You must edit the relationship to see if the cascade delete or update options are selected.

### Cascading Changes and Deletes

Access provides the ability to "Cascade Update Related Fields" and "Cascade Deleted Records". If your relationships are created properly, updating will amount to updating the key field references only in related records of child tables. The cascade delete will cause all related records in child tables to also be deleted. Note: Parent-child relationships are always one-to-many (Parent = 1, Child = $\infty$). While referential integrity can be seen in the relationships window, cascade features are only visible when viewing the properties of a relationship.

## Data Flow Diagrams (MCSD)

Data flow diagrams may appear in a variety of simple ways. For example, a data flow diagram may be a simple procedure by which information is handled in an office: Secretary 1 receives a fax, determines who should see it first, then delivers. Let us say it is an order, so it goes to the next available salesperson. The salesperson verifies availability with the warehouse, who in turn updates their order. After verification, management approves the sale and it becomes an order. The order clerk gathers the materials and delivers them to shipping, etc.

This is a simple example of a common workplace. Data flow diagramming is fundamentally the same in computers, in terms of data workflow. We can draw it up just like a flowchart, or we can be less glamorous and use plain text with arrows, or plain boxes containing text with arrows.

In terms of data connectivity, data flow diagrams become high-level diagrams illustrating how various sources of data are connected. The easiest way to think of this is in terms of a relational database (see normalizing and denormalizing). Let us say, for example, we are trying to create a high-level diagram illustrating the data flow of a school's database. The following may be a logical arrangement for our data flow:

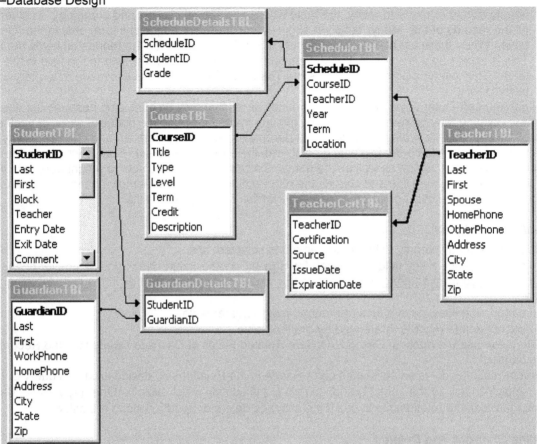

This layout allows for one teacher to have many classes, for many teachers to teach the same class, for many students to have the same parents, and many students to take the same class, etc. This diagram is a massive simplification though. As a rule, I put all people into one table with a field distinguishing who belongs to which category. As a consequence, if this were a working diagram, Teacher, Student, and Guardian would be queries and not tables. This diagram gives us a good idea of the concepts though, and can be extremely useful in development (e.g. making the denormalization observation I just made). Diagrams like this can also help solve problems in design. For example, I went to a friend's house for dinner one night to help him with a database problem. We struggled for hours examining the innermost design of the programming. Finally, as dinner was about to be served, I printed out the relationships. As I waited to be served, I looked at the diagram and sipped my soda. Suddenly the problem leaped out at me: he was trying to use a relational database like a flat table. He had put calculations into the tables rather than into the queries. I leaped from my seat, and before my dinner had a chance to cool, the database was working.

## Integrity and Validation (MCSD)

The largest problems with integrity and validation are the users and the available information. By more fields required in a record, the less user-friendly it will be. It will result in a shortage of information in many instances. For example, in a database designed for a private college, I was tempted to make contact information and social security numbers required fields. Unfortunately, in the working environment, much of this information filters into the database months after the student has already begun. Rather than have no information, only the First and Last name fields are required. This, of course, deeply affects the integrity of the database.

Validation can be worked to extremes. Some databases are set so the user's input is compared with known information, requiring accuracy and validity in input. This can make a database enormously cumbersome, and risks a user being unable to make input of unknown information impossible. Validation with numeric data is more practical (see Input Masks, Lookup Fields, Constraints and Validation in this unit).

## Integrating Business Rules (MCSD)

Business rules may require additional fields in tables. For example, you can create a lookup for grades that applies numeric values to the letters, and numeric values for credit hours or contact hours applied to the course. The problem with these values comes when you calculate GPAs. For example: 4 = A, 3 = B, 2 = C, 1 = D, 0 = F, 5 = Z (not passing), 6 = P (pass), 7 = I (incomplete), 8 = AU (audit). The values 0 thru 4 are useful for computing GPA, but 5 thru 8 are not counted. These business rules can be either inserted directly into the programming, or a table must be created using these key values and two binary (Yes/No) fields: Count Credit Hours, and Count Toward GPA. 0 thru 4 and 6 would be true for Count Credit Hours. Only 0 thru 4 would be true for Count Toward GPA.

### Notes:

When the business rules are programmed in, then the user has no power.
When the business rules are accessible because they are not programmed in, then security measures must exist to protect the rules from users who do not have authority over them.
By not programming business rules in, the program is more user friendly and adaptable, making the client less dependant on the programmer.

## Math on The Computer

This lesson assumes minimal knowledge of mathematics and maximum aversion to mathematics. Mathematics, like technology, is commonly shrouded by anxieties and fears. Mathematicians are guaranteed solitude simply by mentioning their field. As we realized in our Windows unit, these enchanting chalk circles are nothing more than boundaries we create. Mathematics is remarkably easy if approached positively and concretely.
It is not the objective here to replace traditional math classes. Nor is it our objective to delve into manipulations nor calculations. The idea of this lesson is to show the non-mathematician how to get the computer to do the math for them. As with reading, writing and computer literacy, mathematics is a necessity. Fortunately computer literacy can easily substitute for mathematical literacy when applied to common and most advanced math needs.
The computer can easily and instantly track many related mathematical operations consisting of many values each which would baffle even the math connoisseur. The way software is designed, you basically need to know:
1. The values you want calculated
2. The manner of calculation (often this does not mean the formula)
3. How you want the results to appear
Mathematics on the computer also includes operations we forget are math-related. For example, counting occurrences, or making decisions. In the process of our daily lives we perform enormously complex mathematical operations constantly. For example, as we drive down the road we unconsciously calculate distances, speed and velocities, then make decisions based on values we did not consciously apply numbers to. What is even more remarkable: we make these calculations in a fraction of a second. If we don't, then paramedics may get involved. On a less drastic level, we shop. Shopping alone is an enormous math problem. Do I have this? Will I need more? How many? Can I afford it? In comparison, the math we do on the computer is insignificant and simple. The difference is that we are trying to formally calculate actual values. The irony is we can easily describe actual values because we can physically show and measure them. Most of the values we risk our lives on are so abstract we cannot give a real value to them. For example: food likes and dislikes. We might absolutely love some foods and absolutely hate

others. Most get valued in a gray area between where we couldn't possibly give a constant value. One day you might crave vegetables, the next cheese. When given other choices our craving could instantly change. Try putting numbers to values like these and you will get a headache. Try counting the apples in a bowl and, assuming none are added nor removed, the number is the same later. Formal math is easy.

## *Numbers*

We humans have a few nasty habits. Among these includes applying abstract numbers to things that have nothing to do with real value. The computer assumes all numbers are values unless told otherwise. Even worse, computers assign numeric value to non-numbers (like the alphabet), which do not always agree with human logic. In our Windows project we organized folders labeled u007, u01, u02, u03, etc. You probably wondered why the extra zero. We ignore zeros to the left of the number we are treating as a value. When it comes to alphabetizing, the computer considers the value of each character in order. Punctuation has less value than numbers (0-9 mind you!). Numbers have less value than letters. We organize numbers by their value rather than one character at a time, such as: 1, 2, 3, 4, 5, 6, 7, 8, 9, 10, 11, 20. The computer, with the same series of numbers will show: 1, 10, 11, 2, 20, 3, 4, 5, 6, 7, 8, 9. To get the computer to sort properly (treating numbers as text), add a zero on the left of the single digits: 01, 02, 03, 04, 05, 06, 07, 08, 09, 10, 11, 20. Conceptions and applications of numbers as text and values is a problem.

To further complicate numbers, we have numbers that we never calculate like: area codes, zip codes, bar codes, customer numbers, vendor and employee numbers. We treat these as text while the computer easily conceives them as calculable values. Then we throw characters into numbers that are for human use only but, to the computer, serve mathematical purposes such as: dashes (-), commas and slashes (/). While data entry methods resolve this last issue, when facing a spreadsheet or database you must tell the computer the type of information it is storing in that place to prevent confusing values with text. In research, to insure consistency of data entry, numbers are often assigned to non-calculable characteristics, like sex, religion and ethnicity. Clearly these values cannot be used to calculate sums, averages, etc. The values are descriptive so we can count them and compare the counts. Likewise a file could be active or inactive, present or not present. These yes/no scenarios are easily counted and compared, though the numbers assigned to them are nothing more than qualitative identifiers (numeric labels).

## *Variables*

There are a number of ways too look at variables which all fall into one of two categories: qualitative or quantitative. Take an eight ounce (half pint) cup out of your cupboard and consider what you can fill it with. The size of the cup is actually a factor of its volume, which happens to be sized to fit eight ounces of water at room temperature. What you put into the cup must naturally fit, such as grains, powders and liquids, and the weights of your choices differ per unit of volume. This describes a qualitative variable because the nature of the filling material can vary. Just because it is an eight ounce cup does not mean you have to fill the entire volume, hence the quantity put into the cup also can vary (to the size limitation of the cup of course). What confuses people the most is when mathematicians convert this concept into letters or symbols. For simplicity sake we will use the letter V to denote the volume of the cup, W for the weight of the filling, Y the volume quantity of the filling and X the quality of the filling (the type of filling (T) and its weight (W) per unit of volume (a constant 1) or X=WT/1). If we fill the cup with X then necessarily Y=V. We note that V is a constant so long as we use the same container, and that XY gives us the weight of the filling so long as Y is less than or equal to V. If Y exceeds V, we need a bigger container (V). This is fundamentally how mathematicians use symbols to represent reality and all the variations of reality. Fortunately for the non-mathematician, the layout of a spreadsheet makes variables a little easier to comprehend. Each cell represents a variable. Until filled, the cell has a null (or empty) value. A null value is different from a zero value. Zero is a measure of a thing (namely the absence of that thing). A null value is the absence of anything. You note the primary difference is that zero is used for a particular quality, while null lacks even quality and hence cannot be measured. When the cell is filled, the nature of the variable within the cell is obvious. It is either a number or text, then formatted to best represent the quality of the variable (percent, currency, etc.). The reference to the cell is the location of the cell, so the user is not just considering loosely defined letters, but places that they can look at and see actual data. Cell references (locations) are defined first by the column letter than by the row number. This is no accident of ordering nor of choice to make columns letters and rows numbers. Columns represent the X axis of mathematics which is graduated (numbered) from left to right horizontally. Rows represent the Y axis of mathematics which is graduated (numbered) from bottom to top vertically. Because we read and write from the top of the page down, spreadsheets reverse the row numbering system. As for using letters and numbers, not only does this help the user better understand the reference, it simplifies the naming system. In mathematics coordinates are given as (X,Y) while coordinates of a cell in a spreadsheet are provide CR (column letter then row number) which is considerably fewer characters yet equally descriptive for the application. If there could be fractions of cells, this reference system would not work. Fortunately this is not the case.

Both numbers and text can be variable or constant. If we select a cell and input a number or text, then we have put a constant in the variable space of the cell. If we use a formula using references to other cells, then what is displayed becomes variable and dependent on the contents of other cells. Although you can refer to cells containing formulas, eventually all higher order formulas must refer to constants that dictate their solutions. If formulas only refer to each other and no constants are referred to, than a circular relationship (argument) exists and there can be no solution.

## Conditional Operators

| | |
|---|---|
| = | States equality between the two sides. Note: all Excel and Access formulas and logical expressions begin with this symbol! It tells the program to display the solution in the cell rather than the formula. |
| <> | States that the two sides are not equal. |
| < | States the value on the left is less than the value on the right. |
| <= | States the value on the left is less than or equal to the value on the right. |
| > | States the value on the left is greater than the value on the right. |
| >= | States the value on the left is greater than or equal to the value on the right. |

# Worksheet 7—Database Design

<u>Tough Stuff</u>

## Tables (some answers used more than once)

1. System of table design where tables with few records are associated with variable length tables of information where multiple records provide greater definition to individual records in the other table.
2. Always divide these into their smallest logical parts to distinguish between specific data items.
3. Type of database where tables with different information can share that information with each other.
4. A setting established between two tables to indicate that they share information.
5. Carefully manage the sizes of these to prevent unnecessary inflation consuming memory resources.
6. One or more data items defining qualities of one or more unique key names.
7. An area defining the qualities of the data, how it is inputted, shown and stored.

   a. Field
   b. Record
   c. Relational
   d. Hierarchy
   e. Relationship

## Table Classifications and Types I  (some answers used more than once)

8. Type of table that always has a key field.
9. A table with no ancestry nor descendents (contains all data) where key fields are optional and composite keys may even be a necessity.
10. Any table with ancestry.
11. Any table with descendents.
12. A table with ancestry but no descendents (gets data from other tables but gives no data to other tables).
13. Type of table that never has a key field.
14. Special function table containing data used in Module processes (convention: *TableNamePTBL*).

   a. Child
   b. Flat
   c. Parent
   d. Procedural
   e. Terminal

## Table Classifications and Types II

15. A table with multiple ancestors forming a relationship that would otherwise not be possible.
16. A table providing variable quantities of details describing qualities of its ancestors.
17. Table with descendents but no ancestors.
18. A table with at least one ancestor with changing information based on a value such as a date.
19. Special function table containing only a single record typically constrained so all fields are lookups to fields in other tables or queries. This type helps users quickly locate data on forms and print reports.

   a. Characteristic
   b. History
   c. Associative
   d. Navigation
   e. Kernel

## Relationships (some answers used more than once)

20. A relationship specifying that all records in one table (where the arrow points away from) will be shown in queries, forms and reports using multiple tables and/or queries as data sources, even if there are no matching records in the other table (where the arrow points to).
21. A relationship that causes only related records to be shown in queries, forms and reports using multiple tables and/or queries as data sources.
22. Provides options to update fields in related tables or delete records in child tables when a parent record is deleted.
23. Shown in the relationships window with 1 and ∞ (many) on the connecting lines.
24. Only visible in the properties of a relationship.
25. Protects data by forbidding: changing data referenced from another table, deleting records referenced by another table, or changing a key field referenced from or by another table.
26. An outer join that requires many-to-many relationships (see Third Normal Form), appropriately used between a child table and a query made of its parent that shows all child records even if they do not have matching records in the query.
27. Shown with an arrow pointing to the child table indicating all parent records will be shown.

   a. Outer Join
   b. Right Outer Join
   c. Left Outer Join
   d. Inner Join
   e. Referential Integrity
   f. Cascading

## Special Data Types (some answers used more than once)

28. Always attach this to the key field of another table, even if you show other data instead.
29. Field data type where data input is done using a combination box or radio button group.
30. A field sorted and indexed (No Duplicates) unique to each record, or if multiple fields are used, the combination of the fields cannot be replicated and the first is always sorted.. This is used to identify records and find information quickly (e.g. with a binary search algorithm).
31. An unsorted field whose data is replicated elsewhere in a sorted form to enable quickly searching for data in that field. These should be used sparingly.
32. Provides a fixed list of options stored in the table's design for the user to choose from.
33. Binary data type where data input is done with either a checkbox or toggle button.
34. Provides a list of options stored in another table or query design for the user to choose from.

   a. Embedded Lookup
   b. Linked Lookup
   c. All Lookups
   d. Yes/No
   e. Key
   f. Index (Duplicates OK)

## Miscellaneous

| | | |
|---|---|---|
| 35. Term used to describe the definition of a field which includes all the field qualities such as formatting, data type, input masks, indexing, and validation. | a. | Conventions |
| 36. Name extensions used to easily differentiate objects such as: Table (TBL), Query (QRY), Form (FRM), Macro (MCR), and Module (MOD) | b. | Expressions |
| | c. | Masks |
| 37. Forbidden in names of fields, tables, queries, expressions, macros, groups and modules. | d. | Normal Forms |
| 38. Formulas that should almost always be constructed in queries. | e. | Shapes |
| 39. Development rules for relationships and data storage to manage decomposable data. | f. | Spaces |
| 40. Rules created by the developer governing how data is put into a field and what is stored. | | |

## Query Types

| | | |
|---|---|---|
| 41. Type of query that performs calculations (sum, count, average, variance, standard deviation, minimum and maximum) on ranges of data | a. | Append |
| 42. Action query that modifies the information in one or more fields based on criteria. | b. | Crosstab |
| 43. Action query or import option that inserts data from one source to the end of another table. | c. | Select |
| 44. Type of query that can make computations and show data from one or more tables or queries in accordance with their relationships and stated criteria. | d. | Summary |
| | e. | Update |
| 45. Type of query providing values (which may be computed) in a column and row layout whose labels are typically derived from related tables. Useful in showing history and detail values. | | |

## Useful Languages

| | | |
|---|---|---|
| 46. A language used to build control structure libraries for use in other programs. | a. | SQL |
| 47. A dynamic language capable of providing a complete interface for input and output (forms and reports) containing the coding of other languages for background control features. | b. | Visual Basic (VB) |
| | c. | Visual Basic for Applications (VBA) |
| 48. Language capable of building tables, extracting and manipulating data, but does not provide user-friendly interface features. | d. | Macro |
| 49. Language used in Access modules to customize the interface and data control. | e. | ActiveX |
| 50. A sequence of predefined actions used to perform simple tasks when a specific event occurs such as the clicking of a button or the changing of information in a field on a form | | |

## Easy Stuff

### Hierarchy of a Database

| | | |
|---|---|---|
| 51. Contains a group of items defining a key field (e.g. a name) | a. | Relational |
| 52. Contains a group of one or more characters | b. | Table |
| 53. Contains a group of binary (0 or 1) numbers defining a character | c. | Record |
| 54. Contains a group of names with similar characteristics | d. | Field |
| 55. Contains two or more groups with at least one characteristic in common | e. | Byte |

### Styles

| | | |
|---|---|---|
| 56. 12.000 | a. | Comma |
| 57. $12,000.00 | b. | Currency |
| 58. Basic style applied to values | c. | Decimal |
| 59. .002 | d. | Number |
| 60. 12% | e. | Percent |

### Data Types

| | | |
|---|---|---|
| 61. Setting used for a field where most entries will have the same value | a. | Autonumber |
| 62. Use this type when only one of two values are possible | b. | Default |
| 63. Used for basic values | c. | Number |
| 64. Great for making a key field | d. | Memo |
| 65. Use for lengthy text up to 65,535 characters (Text type only contains 255 characters) | e. | Yes/No |

### Controls (letters used more than once)

| | | | |
|---|---|---|---|
| 66. Put field information here | 70. Put Expressions here | a. | Radio Button |
| 67. Use this to annotate (make notes not in the database) | 71. Any combination in a group may be selected | b. | Label |
| | 72. One of a group of these must be selected | c. | Data (Textbox) |
| 68. Field with multiple lines that may be scrolled through to see choices | 73. Drops down to show choices | d. | Checkbox |
| | 74. Put automatic text (e.g. page #) here | e. | Combination Box |
| 69. Put Yes/No data types here | 75. Put field label/name here | | |

### Expressions

| | | |
|---|---|---|
| 76. Pre-defined function | a. | =iif(<arg>,<truepart>,<falsepart>) |
| 77. Table/Query reference | b. | [Company] |
| 78. User-defined Function | c. | [South]! |
| 79. Logical Argument | d. | =count([grade]) |
| 80. Field Reference | e. | ([unit1] + [unit2]) / 200 |

### Arguments

| | | |
|---|---|---|
| 81. 4 ___ 3 | a. | = |
| 82. 3 ___ 4 | b. | < |
| 83. 3 ___ 3 | c. | <= |
| 84. If X=3 or 4, X ___ 4 | d. | > |
| 85. If X=3 or 4, X ___ 3 | e. | >= |

www.ingramcontent.com/pod-product-compliance
Lightning Source LLC
Chambersburg PA
CBHW080421060326

40689CB00019B/4322